100 PER CENT MIND POWER

Learn how to tap the creative
power of the mind

100 PER CENT MIND POWER

The Psychogenesis Way

Jack Ensign Addington

EXCALIBUR
BOOKS

First published in the USA by Dodd, Mead & Company, Inc.,
New York, 1971
This edition published 1988

British Library Cataloguing in Publication Data

Addington, Jack Ensign
    100 per cent mind power:
    the psychogenesis way.
    1. Self-realization   2. Psychical
    research
    I. Title
    131   BF637.S4

    ISBN 0-85454-087-3

*Excalibur is an imprint of the Thorsons Publishing Group,
Wellingborough, Northamptonshire, NN8 2RQ, England.*

Printed in Great Britain by Billing & Sons Limited, Worcester

10   9   8   7   6   5   4   3   2

To my wife, Cornelia, whose inspiration, dedication and loving cooperation made this book possible

We have been following the successive stages of the same grand progression from the fluid contours of the early earth. Beneath the pulsations of geo-chemistry, of geo-tectonics and of geo-biology, we have detected one and the same fundamental process, always recognisable—the one which was given material form in the first cells and was continued in the construction of nervous systems. We saw geogenesis promoted to biogenesis, which turned out in the end to be nothing else than psychogenesis.

Teilhard de Chardin, *The Phenomenon of Man*

. . . the action of thought-power is not limited to a circumscribed individuality.

What the individual does is to give direction to something which is unlimited, to call into action a force infinitely greater than his own, which because it is in itself impersonal though intelligent, will receive the impress of his personality, and can therefore make its influence felt far beyond the limits which bound the individual's objective perception of the circumstances with which he has to deal.

Thomas Troward, *Edinburgh Lectures*

THE STARTING POINT

AN INTRODUCTION TO A NEW LIFE

Sɪxᴛᴇᴇɴ ʏᴇᴀʀs spent in the business world as a practicing attorney, plus twenty years in the ministry have taught me one thing—man is his own worst enemy.

It would be safe to say that during this time I have counseled with well over twenty thousand troubled people. Each one thought that his problem was unique; yet, in my eyes, each one had the same problem. Each one had, in some way, underrated himself and his capacity to succeed in life; each one had failed to direct his own mind into right avenues that would bring him fulfillment; each one thought that life was against him when the truth was, he was against himself.

I discovered that there was a law of mind that worked in every instance if the person involved was willing to give it a try. Whenever a person was willing to change his thinking, giving new conscious direction to his subconscious mind, there was an immediate change in his outer experience. William James had discovered this before the turn of the century when he said that every thought was motor in its consequences; but this had been little understood by most people.

Once I had discovered the tremendous power hidden within the subconscious mind and learned how to use it, I was no longer content to help people resist each other in court. I was drawn into the ministry where I found that I could give them far better help.

I began to keep track of the steady stream of people who passed through my office, of the constant telephone calls and letters from people who sought a better life expression. Soon my files were bulging with case histories, letters, reports of grateful people who had found that there was something that they could do to better their conditions. I call these files my "demonstration files" for they portray wonderful demonstrations of the power of mind at work.

Through my work with people, I have developed the science of Self-Direction—the art of directing the subconscious mind into channels of right use. There is no longer any doubt in my mind about the effectiveness of this science. *That which a person believes about himself, that which he confidently expects and anticipates, will become his experience.* There is a definite and readily applied system of Self-Direction that can meet every problem known to man. This is a universe of law and order. Every part of life is governed by law. Nothing depends upon chance or environment. Everything in the outer world can be overcome through the working of the mind. Every problem has an answer through Self-Direction. The key is Psychogenesis, *everything begins in mind.* It didn't happen just once in the beginning of the world: life is continually re-creating itself. We are constantly beginning again —and it is through Mind that all of this takes place. *In the beginning, Mind created the heaven and the earth.* Each new concept that we place in mind takes form as a completely new sequence of happenings in our experience.

In this book I have endeavored to present answers to some of the most common problems that have been presented to me, problems that have been overcome at one time or another by people with whom I have worked, with the hope that now many more people can be helped through Self-Direction.

The law that we use in Self-Direction is this: *Every thought*

that one consciously thinks makes an impression on the sub-
conscious mind that will express itself as action according to
the strength and the desire contained within the thought.

We all need to learn how to clean up the subconscious
mind, rooting out of it the things that we do not choose to
experience. We need to prove that we can take dominion of
our thinking, thereby taking dominion over our lives; that
we can give the orders to our own subconscious minds and
know that they will be precisely executed with the cooperation of all of the power and wisdom of the Universe. Self-
Direction is the art of redirecting the subconscious mind in
a positive way, knowing that mind will follow through and
carry out our positive directions. Psychogenesis is the principle—everything begins in mind—Self-Direction is the way
to use it.

I offer you now the opportunity to become the master of
your fate. Through an understanding of Psychogenesis, it is
simpler than you may think. It makes no difference whether
you are a housewife, a businessman, a salesman, a teacher, or
a student. Once you understand how to use Psychogenesis,
through Self-Direction, you can learn to relax at will, overcome any bad habit pattern that bothers you, sleep like a
baby, get along better with others, have a happy marriage,
and succeed beyond your fondest dreams in everything you
undertake.

JACK ENSIGN ADDINGTON

CONTENTS

I EVERYTHING BEGINS
IN MIND

> *In the beginning God created the heaven and the
> earth. And the earth was without form, and void; and
> darkness was upon the face of the deep. And the Spirit of
> God moved upon the face of the waters.*
>
> GENESIS 1:1, 2

PSYCHOGENESIS, *mind + a beginning*, means *everything begins in mind.* In the beginning Mind created the heaven and
the earth. Mind is all there is. What appears as the body of
life is the everchanging creation of Mind. Does this surprise
you? Think a moment. Everything we see about us had to
be first an idea in Mind. Each one of us is an idea in the Universal Mind. We may think of ourselves as separate and apart
from life, but we are actually as much a part of the One Mind
as a drop of water in the ocean is one with the sea.

The world and all that it contains is made up of ideas
made manifest. The manifest, or physical universe, is really
only the afterglow, the lingering evidence of that which has
already taken place in Mind. That which the world calls real
had to have started with psychogenesis. It had to have a beginning in the invisible world of Mind. Whether we like it
or not, this is a mental world.

The automobile you drive, the house in which you live,
the chair upon which you are sitting were first an idea in
Mind. It all was first visualized in Mind and then came into
being through the creative process of Mind.

"But," you say, "how about my physical body, how about the tree I see from my window, I didn't think of them. They were not in my mind before they came into being."

MIND IS INFINITE

The fallacy here is to think that Mind is contained within the brain of man. The human brain is but an instrument of Mind. The orderly arrangement of the manifest universe proves that there is an Intelligence that is Universal, an Intelligence that exists within the atom and is reproduced in and through every part of life extending into the infinite Universe. There is no place where this Intelligence does not exist. All is Mind and the creation of Mind.

This morning I cut a papaya in half. Is there anything more beautiful than the inside of a papaya? It is apricot in color with the texture of satin and only the Master Artist could have planned the lovely contrast of those shiny black seeds. How many seeds do you suppose there are in a papaya? Someday I am going to count them! Such abundance! Each seed capable of producing unlimited fruit. Oh, the abundance of Life! It was planned that way. If one seed was lost, there were many more so that some would be sure of reproducing themselves in the continuing life of the fruit. An Intelligence so great that it is beyond our comprehension planned it that way. Each tiny detail of life precisely planned to dovetail with all the rest of life, each making its contribution to the universal whole.

Did you ever watch the common housefly groom himself? It is fascinating to see. He lifts his dainty little legs and places them on top of his wings. Under those legs are fine hairs that act as soft brushes. Again and again he gently strokes his gossamer wings. These delicate wings would be severely hampered by even a particle of dust. The brushing of the wings must be a very important interlude in the day of a fly. Did the fly's mother teach him to polish his wings with such painstaking care? Who taught the first fly this process of grooming? Mind planned it all, down to the insignificant housefly with his lovely bottle-green wings and his intricate system of aerodynamics! Surely there must be a Master Intelligence behind it all, an all-knowing Mind permeating all of life.

How else could you account for the perfect balance that exists between the various activities of the human body. What a masterful job the Great Engineer did in interrelating the various organs, glands, and functions of the body, so that one gland would be able to take over the work of another that is not performing properly; or, the body, without our taking conscious thought, can provide for various emergencies and even compensate for our misuse of it! Has there ever been a machine to compare with it? No, never. Man has failed to produce a robot to replace himself because of one element— the interrelating activity of the Universal Mind.

Examining the intricate design of the Universe, man must ask himself, "How could anyone believe that it all just happened without a Master Mind behind it?" How can we separate this Master Mind from any part of its creation? It is man's failing that he continually takes the miracle of Life for granted, or, thinking he must prop it up, endeavors to change and improve upon a design that is already faultless.

MAN IS GIVEN DOMINION

Where, then, is man given the opportunity to create? It is in the area of individual creativity that man has been given the privilege to make choices, the authority to direct his own thoughts and express the ideas that come to him. Man has been made cocreator with the Universal Mind in the area of his own life. Here, according to the divine plan, he is given dominion. The creative process of life gives him the authority to direct the events that take place in his experience.

The Psalmist puts it this way: *Thou madest him to have dominion over the works of thy hands; thou hast put all things under his feet.*

If we do not like the world that we have created for ourselves, we have been given the privilege of creating a new one by making a new mold, or mental equivalent, from which to start a new chain of events more to our liking. This is Self-Direction. We create the mental mold, and Mind goes to work at once to fill it for us. Once we understand how Mind works, we are able to trust it.

MIND IS BOTH DIRECTOR AND PRODUCER

When Universal Mind created man in its own image, it shared with him the power to create. *Male and female created He them.* The male aspect of life is the conscious, directive mind within each one of us. The female aspect is the feminine mind, the subconscious, receptive, creative medium within each one of us. In other words, there is only one mind, with two aspects, the conscious and subconscious use of the mind. It doesn't matter whether you are a man or a woman, each one of us uses the masculine, directive mind and each uses the feminine, creative aspect of mind. Through the dual function of mind, we have been given dominion over our lives. We use the omnipotent Power of Universal Mind at our own point of awareness. There is no other power.

TO MAN IS GIVEN THE CHALLENGE

This is the one Mind common to all individual men described by Emerson and each man is an inlet and an outlet to it. Each one of us has access to the universal storehouse of Wisdom, of Understanding, and Intelligence. An infinite

Source of ideas is available to us. Emerson also said, every inspiration is an influx of the Divine Mind into our mind, the key to man is his thought. It is through ideas that the Divine Mind continues its creation through man. The mind of man is the mouth of God.

Everything needed by man already exists for him in the Universal Mind. As he becomes receptive and learns how to be open to the influx of the Divine Mind, he is able to take the ideas that come and put them to use, choosing from among them the direction he would like to follow. Man does not have to be a pawn of fate, to be blown by winds of chance in one direction and then another. He can chart his course according to the orderly planning of the Universal Intelligence. What a magnificent challenge has been given to man, the opportunity to take dominion of his life! But with it is given the responsibility of using intelligently the infinite resources of life.

HOW ONE WOMAN TOOK DOMINION IN HER LIFE

I once counseled with a woman who had spent her life living in an atmosphere of stress and negation. Laura admitted that all her life she had felt guilty about nearly everything she thought or did. She came to me because her husband had divorced her with no forewarning. She was desperate. She told me that this had been a great shock to her.

"I never thought that it would happen," were her words.

In the next breath, she admitted that she was a very impressionable person; that whenever she heard of a divorce, she had immediately thought, "What would happen to me if my husband ever divorced me?" In her mind, she had entertained this possibility many times, suffering each time the horrors of rejection and loneliness. It turned out that she had had this deep-seated fear for many years, even though she had told me at first that she had never thought it would happen. Even though there was no evidence in the marriage to support this underlying fear, it was a case of, as Job put it, *the thing which I greatly feared is come upon me.*

She began to see that she had been mentally going in two directions at once. Consciously, she claimed that she had not thought of divorce, but subconsciously, she was filled with fear of divorce. In the deep, feeling part of the mind, she had not only accepted divorce as a possibility but had unwittingly given that direction to the mind which had ultimately become her experience.

Laura and I agreed that it was now necessary for her to build a new mental house. Applying the principle of Psychogenesis, she must now develop an entirely new approach to life in order to make a new mental beginning. It was a large order. She said that she hardly knew where to start. I suggested she go to a stationer and buy herself a large composition book. In it, she was to write down her negative thoughts as she became aware of them. Afterwards, she was to analyze these negative thoughts and see how she could translate them into their positive counterpart. We also agreed that every time she felt guilty about something, she should write down this feeling in her journal. Each guilt could then be turned around and made a point of self-acceptance, rather than a point of self-condemnation.

Several weeks went by. When she brought her notebook in, we discussed some of the negative thoughts she had written in it. She began to see that she habitually entertained negative responses toward almost everything that happened in her life. For instance, when her attorney had suggested that she invest in the stock market, she immediately assumed that this would mean throwing the money away. When friends, hoping a change of scenery would cheer her, suggested that she go on a trip, all she could think of was the possibility of an accident. As for a new marriage, she admitted that her reaction had been, "I'll never marry again. A long, lonely life stretches out ahead of me."

And now, as she read to me from her notebook, Laura began to laugh. "How could I have been so negative!"

Together we worked out a new, positive plan of Self-Direction. This was the framework for a new mental house. She began to see that it was just as easy to approach life in a positive manner as in a negative manner and much more productive. The notebook proved very revealing. I recommend this system to you if you would like to sort out your undesirable thoughts from your worthwhile thinking. As Laura remarked one day, "If the thoughts I put into mind are going to become my experience, I had better start putting into mind that which I would like to experience."

I wish that I could tell you that the new mental house was furnished and ready to move into then and there. It was not quite that simple. It took some doing to dismantle the old one. Laura did not, one day, have a notebook filled with negative responses and on the next, a beautiful, new, affirmative approach. There were many weeds in her thought garden and they were not rooted out overnight. There were old fears to be disposed of, old guilts that had put down taproots deep in the subconscious mind.

There was, for instance, the thought that life had passed her by, that there would never be another opportunity to marry. It was hard for her to forgive herself for past failure. She had, in her youth, been a famous dancer. It was hard to believe that some hidden talent could be uncovered and developed today.

WORKING FROM THE FINISHED PICTURE

So, we set up a list of new goals and started out working from what I call *the finished picture*. Instead of thinking about the loneliness today, the feelings of guilt and inadequacy, she started giving her whole attention to the kind of life she would like to be living. Whenever old negative responses presented themselves, they were met with positive responses which, little by little, began to neutralize the old negative patterns. The affirmative approaches grew stronger and finally overcame the negative patterns.

Laura listed these goals in the back of her composition book:

1. Self-expression
2. Companionship
3. A happy marriage

Today, I am happy to say, they have all been realized. At the time she first wrote them down, she said they all seemed impossible.

Now, she is an accomplished artist, having taken up oil painting with all of the zest she once put into dancing. Recently, I was invited to a one-man show of her work and noted that most of the paintings were marked "sold." Her work is receiving a great deal of attention, is actually in demand. Once she got her mind off herself and her problems, it turned out that she was very good company. Through her work, she has made many friends in art circles, friends who share her interests. You might say, her second goal was realized as a by-product of her first goal.

In the course of her work, she met another artist, a widower who was attracted to her by her beautiful paintings.

"I've got to know that person," he remarked to a friend. "She paints as if she loves life. There is so much joy in her work; she must be a wonderful person."

They met and were drawn to each other on sight. Within six months they were married, and they tell me, "This is a marriage that *was* made in heaven."

And, now, the third goal was realized. I wish that I could show you before and after pictures of Laura. Today, she is not the same woman I first knew. There is no looking backward now, no bitterness or self-condemnation. When she made over her mental house, she remade her world in every way. The goals that she set up for herself were the mental molds we were talking about. The Universal Mind filled them, every one.

II HOW SELF-DIRECTION WORKS

Thought precedes action as lightning does thunder.

HEINRICH HEINE

D<small>ID</small> you ever hear of a garlic detective? One of my best friends, who passed on a few years ago, was a garlic detective. She was always looking for garlic, not because she loved it, but because she hated it so much. To her it was public enemy number one. I often wondered if it wasn't a case of "which came first, the chicken or the egg." Did she hate garlic first? Or, did she eat it in some concoction that seemed not to agree with her and ever after the memory of that experience caused her to feel that she was allergic to garlic? At any rate, it became a source of great concern to her. Someone would suggest that a group go out to dinner and the usual discussion would ensue. A friend would say, "We could go to that nice little French restaurant, or how about Italian food tonight?" And then everyone would turn to Alice and she would say:

"We'd better not try anything foreign like that. I always find it's safer to stick to the places where they serve good, plain American food. They are apt to have garlic in those foreign places."

We would be very careful when she came to our house for dinner not to rub the salad bowl with garlic. We'd even read the fine print on the bottle of prepared dressing just to be sure there wasn't a little garlic powder in it. We knew that if there was, our garlic detective would soon discover it. Often, she would accuse us of trying to trap her so that we could prove that it was all in her mind. Because she was such a good friend, this was always playfully done—sort of kidding on the square, you know. She would say to us: "I know you folks like garlic. I'll bet you've put it in something tonight."

She expected it everywhere she went. She worried about it. Often she got it. And then she would be sick. Sometimes the restaurant would assure her that there was no garlic in their food, but if there was, she would detect it and pay the price in suffering later. The interesting thing was that sometimes, even if there wasn't any garlic used, she would still become ill. The very thought of garlic made her sick. As you can imagine, this became quite a problem to her through the years.

THE SUBCONSCIOUS MIND—THE BUILDER OF THE BODY

The subconscious mind has been called the builder of the body. It runs the body's functions in an automatic way. The *great involuntary life* goes on whether we are awake or asleep. Isn't it fortunate that the Master Planner arranged it so? What a chore it would be if we had to give instructions to the heart to keep it beating, to the stomach every time we wanted some food digested, to the blood to keep it circulating? No, everything is done for us in a wonderful way. All bodily growth, every function of the body, stems from the subconscious mind. There actually is intelligence within every cell and every atom of the body, and this intelligence is tied to the subconscious mind.

THE SUBCONSCIOUS MIND REASONS DEDUCTIVELY

The subconscious mind can reason only deductively. The conscious mind gives the orders, the subconscious mind goes to work to carry them out. Deductive reasoning means taking two premises and putting them together and from them drawing a conclusion. This is called a syllogism, which the dictionary defines as *a logical form of reasoning, consisting of a major premise, a minor premise, and a conclusion.*

Deductive reasoning is reasoning from general principles, which are established *or assumed,* to specific results. You see, it really doesn't matter if the principles are proven; even assumed principles can be used in drawing a conclusion. To reason in this way is known as syllogizing and that is just what the subconscious mind always does. You can easily see that this form of reasoning is correct only to the degree that the original premises are correct.

For instance, take the classic example: *All Russians are communists. The man who works in the music store is a Russian. Therefore, he must be a communist.* The truth is that only a small fraction of the Russian people are communists. Chances are, the man is not a communist.

THE WILLING SERVANT

The conscious mind gives directions to the subconscious mind. The subconscious mind, reasoning deductively, is able to do only one thing: receive directions and follow them implicitly. That is why it has been called *the willing servant.*

Every order you give, every premise that you establish, every belief you adopt, registers in your subconscious mind. Moreover, the subconscious mind has a memory system that far outdistances the modern day computer. It is like a tape recorder. Every order, every belief, every thought that you think becomes a part of the complete and never-failing memory system of the subconscious mind. Even things you do not think that you remember are safely stored there and can be brought forth at any time.

WE MAKE OUR OWN LAWS

Suppose you once sat before an open window after having perspired freely. The breeze blew over you. At the time it felt good, but you felt a little uneasy because once you had heard that colds come from sitting in drafts. Sure enough, you did get a cold. That cinched it. Ever afterward, you had a law for yourself: *sitting in a draft causes a cold*. This is syllogistic reasoning. *Drafts cause colds. I sat in a draft. Therefore I will have a cold.* The subconscious mind has this carefully stored on its "tape recorder." If you sit in a draft today your subconscious will see that your body responds as per order. Even if you think that you have been in a draft, the subconscious mind will follow through dutifully and provide the cold. It is not the actual sitting in the draft that causes the cold, the belief causes it. The subconscious mind, ever alert, picks the belief up and then the congestion starts in. The subconscious mind does not mean to hurt you, it only knows to follow through with the order that has been given it.

Because it can reason only deductively, it will have to wait until you consciously change the order. In Finland they take hot sauna baths and then roll in the snow with no ill effects. Someday, you may learn that you, through Self-Direction, can change the order that has been given; that through the changing of the belief you need never again be bothered with colds. You may discover that there are people who do not have colds from one year to the next; that they sit in drafts, get overheated, and go out in the cold night air, do whatever they please with no fear of colds. You may become convinced that you, too, can experience this freedom from bondage to colds. When this happens, you will have changed the order that you had previously given to your subconscious mind and it will then follow through on the new basis, giving you an immunity to colds forever.

HOW SELF-DIRECTION WORKS

To go back to our garlic detective—perhaps we now can be more understanding. She had eaten something that made her ill at one time and had associated it with the hated garlic. Ever after she lived with the premise: "garlic makes me sick." Then, when she ate garlic, or even thought that she had, she set up the second premise: "I ate garlic"; with the conclusion, "Therefore, I am sick." The conclusion became a law of action to the subconscious mind. She lived under this rule to the last. It caused her a great deal of concern and misery, not to mention the inconvenience it caused her friends. It was a false premise that could have been changed. Fortunately, as far as her friends were concerned, they loved her so much that they were very tolerant of this idiosyncrasy.

Could this particular problem have been overcome through Self-Direction? Yes; I personally have worked with many people who have set up just such premises and have proceeded to live under the bondage of them until they had become convinced that there was a better way. I have known many people who had set up laws for themselves about various kinds of food. Some had actually gotten to the point that food was their enemy until there was hardly anything left that they could eat. This is a form of self-hypnotism.

MANY PEOPLE HYPNOTIZE THEMSELVES

People hypnotize themselves into accepting needless limitation. A girl just telephoned me to discuss such a problem. To make a long story short, she said that she worked in downtown Los Angeles at present. She liked her work very much and it paid well. However, she has two young children who need her at home and she would like to work closer to her home. A position closer to her home is available to her, but in order to make this move she would have to accept a liberal cut in salary. *She has convinced her subconscious mind that it would be absolutely impossible to find the ideal job in the area of her home.* Several times in our conversation she re-affirmed this law that she has set up for herself. "In order to work near home," she kept saying, "I would have to take work that I do not like at a substantial cut in salary."

I have seen many such cases. I am convinced beyond the shadow of doubt that she could, through Self-Direction, establish a new premise and the subconscious mind would go to work for her to make the new premise appear in her experience. She is laying down the rules. The subconscious mind knows only to obey them.

REMOVING THE BARRIERS THROUGH SELF-DIRECTION

Here are two men who overcame the barriers. The first one was sixty-eight years of age, an architect named Harry who had to retire from his regular work because of a rule in the firm that a man past sixty-five should be put out to pasture. Harry felt that he had much to offer life. He didn't feel old. He didn't want to accept the age law. You see, he had a choice at this point. Which premise would he give to the subconscious mind? Should he accept as a law: "No one ever hires a man past sixty-five. I am past sixty-five; therefore, no one will hire me." Or, should he accept this syllogism? "I still have plenty to offer. There is always room at the top for the one who can produce. Therefore, there is a good job looking for me." Harry chose the latter syllogism.

He said to me one day as we discussed the matter in my office, "I'm not through by a long shot. I don't want to stop working. The State of California is now embarking on a big school building program and I intend to be in on it. I'm a good architect, but they have turned me down because of my age."

"And have you accepted for yourself the idea that a person your age cannot get a job?" I asked him.

"Well," he said, "I've just about accepted it. That's why I'm here. I don't really want to accept this sort of limitation."

This was all that he needed to tell me. "Don't accept it, Harry," I said. "Nothing can limit you but your own thinking. If you don't accept this law for yourself, you are ready to go to work. It is when a person your age accepts the idea that he is too old to get another job that this law goes to work against him. Then, everything works together to see that he does not get a job. You see, we establish the law ourselves. We give it to the subconscious mind and the subconscious mind thinks that it is fulfilling our order when it leads us to one turndown after another."

We talked along this line for several minutes and he agreed not to accept age limitation as a barrier to his getting the right position. There was one thing more that I felt should be clarified.

"Would you be willing to take any good job doing work that is in keeping with your abilities? Would you be happy working for someone other than the State?" I asked him.

"Oh, yes," he said, "I would."

Now, he was free to go anywhere. I suggested that he go ahead and write his friend who was then in one of the state departments and tell him how eager he was to get in on this new project, but to tell him that he was not hanging all of his hopes on this one job.

We had changed the entire approach. We took all anxiety out of the picture. We accepted the premise that there was a right position waiting for him, one that would use his capabilities without anyone thinking of age as being a problem. His subconscious mind now did not have to prove that he couldn't get a job because of his age. The new direction was to prove that age had nothing to do with it.

Almost immediately Harry got a letter back from his friend.

The friend said that he had gone into the architectural department and the very first person he talked to was someone who had known Harry many years before, had known all about his work in the school system. Harry hadn't even known that the man was there. This man said,

"Get him up here right away. We need him. The age rule? We'll waive it!"

Within a few days the man who had come to me with a problem of being too old for the job, was in Sacramento on the architectural staff where he remained for five years, at which time he, of his own volition, retired.

People are always setting up laws for themselves and then railing at life because they have to live under those laws. I know people who think that they can't get a job if they are over forty-five. Somehow or other they manage to go to employers who have firm rules regarding age. Perhaps right down the street there is an opening where the age is never asked, but they will miss this opportunity until the direction given to the subconscious mind is changed.

I know of many examples where changing the thought about barriers changed the experience. Perhaps one of the best, concerns a man whom I knew in Los Angeles. Claude was his name. He worked for the telephone company doing specialized work only offered in that one office. Claude longed to move to San Diego. Over and over, I heard him say, "Of course, this would never be possible because they just don't have my kind of work down there." One day, I said to him, "Why don't you try changing that law you've been accepting for yourself all these years?"

He caught on almost at once. "All right," he said, "I'll set up a new one." He wrote it down just to clinch it in his mind!

"I choose to live in San Diego. There is a good position for me that uses all of my capabilities. Therefore, there is the right position for me in San Diego and I accept it."

Within six months, believe it or not, the telephone company moved his entire department to San Diego. They even paid his moving expenses in the bargain!

USING SELF-DIRECTION IN OTHER AREAS OF LIVING

There are so many different areas in our everyday living where we need to redirect the subconscious mind. I know a man who believed that tomatoes made him sick. He had once eaten too many as a child and his stomach had refused them. Forever after, this became his rule: "Never eat tomatoes. They are hard to digest." Furthermore, he set this law up for his own little son. The youngster loved tomatoes, but alas, they always made him ill.

There are so many other laws that people establish for themselves. There's the woman who always wakes up at three o'clock in the morning; the woman who can't seem to lose weight—she takes off five pounds and then gains them right back again. There's the man who keeps getting fired. Each time he lasts about three months and then he finds some fellow employee who is "just impossible to get along with" and he's out looking for another job, never seeing the pattern.

YOU ALONE GIVE THE ORDERS

You alone give the orders to your subconscious mind. Maybe you think you are in bondage to what someone else thinks about you and accepts for you, but it is only because you have accepted this for yourself. Change the belief and you will change your experience. The most important thing that you can learn in this life is that you alone choose your thoughts and your thoughts shape your world.

SELF-DIRECTION

I realize that I have the right to choose my own thoughts.
I am not bound by anyone else's opinion of me.
No one does my thinking for me unless I let them.
I am choosing for myself thoughts of health, happiness, pros-
    perity, love, and understanding.
Fear and hate have no place in my thinking.
From this moment on I am taking dominion of my life.

III CLAIM IT—
IT'S YOURS!

Sow a thought and reap an act.

ONCE, during my days as a practicing attorney, I drew a will for a woman I shall never forget. When we had finished going over her various bequests, she said something that stuck in my mind. Very deliberately, she made this statement: "Someday," she said, "I'm going to be in a position where someone will carry out my every wish. I shall only have to say 'I want,' and someone will do my bidding."

I believe it was Emerson who said, "Be careful what you pray for, you might get it." This woman got her wish. Some years later I was informed that she had had a stroke and was paralyzed. She spent the rest of her life in bed with people waiting on her hand and foot. Her speech never returned. Until the day she died she was able to utter only two words. They were "I want." When she said, "I want," someone would rush to her side. They would hold up various objects and try to understand what it was she wanted and someone would follow out her desire. When this report came to me shortly before she passed on, I remembered the day that she set the law into motion; the day that I stood by the door, ready to make my departure after drawing up her will and she said, "Someday, I am going to be in a position where someone will carry out my every wish. I shall only have to say 'I want,' and someone will do my bidding."

THAT WHICH IS HIDDEN SHALL BE REVEALED

It seems that what we put into mind, sooner or later comes out. This story is on the humorous side, but I understand that it actually happened. Mrs. Dwight Morrow, the mother of Anne Lindbergh, one day was entertaining Mr. J. P. Morgan, her husband's partner, at tea. Little Anne had never been presented to Mr. Morgan, and so he came by to make that young lady's acquaintance. It seems that Mr. Morgan had a tremendous nose. It was not only bulbous, but red, and dramatically dominated his entire countenance. Knowing the propensity of children to speak out what is on their minds, Mrs. Morrow worried about what Anne might say about Mr. Morgan's big nose. She knew that he was very sensitive on the subject.

Mr. Morgan came into the room and little Anne was introduced to him. They talked for a few moments. With mounting anxiety, Mrs. Morrow noted that Anne kept looking at Mr. Morgan's large nose. Her eyes never left this prominent feature and Mrs. Morrow greatly feared that something would be said. It was therefore with great relief that the time came to send her little daughter upstairs. Anne started toward the door and then stopped and looked back at the nose. She went a little farther and then looked back again. Finally, she went slowly up the stairs. With a deep sigh of relief, Mrs. Morrow turned to Mr. Morgan, the teacup in her hand, and asked, "What will you have in your nose, lemon or cream?"

The attention had been given to *nose,* and that was what came forth. The thing to which we give our attention is the thing that will cause us to react. *For the thing which I greatly feared is come upon me, and that which I was afraid of is come unto me,* mused Job in retrospect.

There is no question but that the activity of mind is such that there is always a continual follow through from the conscious activity into the subconscious and on into visible action. "Whatever we identify ourselves with, we tend to become," wrote Ernest Holmes. "Whatever we think about gradually becomes a subconscious pattern, always tending to manifest itself in our experience."

It is plain to see that we keep placing the orders. It is only after they are delivered that we realize we are not always happy to accept the results which we ourselves placed into mind. *For there is nothing covered that shall not be revealed; neither hid, that shall not be known.*[1] There is a law of life that guarantees that every mental seed that we plant will someday bear fruit. If we do not like the fruit, it behooves us to look to our planting. The law is impersonal and will continue to bring to us that which we desire.

In a letter just received, a woman in New York writes:

"My father was a unionist when unions were not generally accepted. I grew up with this syllogism:

" 'The people of the working class have to struggle and fight for their rights to get enough money to live decently. I am a member of the working class, therefore I have to work awfully hard to make an adequate living.'

"I see now that I have lived under this self-limiting law for the past thirty years. My new syllogism is:

"God is infinite Love, Health, Wisdom and Abundance.

"I am a child of God, made in His image and likeness, therefore I am free, loving, wise, guided in all my ways, and manifest unlimited supply."

This woman has claimed for herself an entirely new approach to life and it is sure to become manifest as improved circumstances.

UNCOVERING THE LAW OF MIND

In this day of great scientific achievement, relatively little attention has been given to a scientific understanding of the mind. A study of philosophy shows us that down through the

[1] Luke 12:2.

ages man has understood many things he has been unable to define. Today these definitions are coming into focus. We are beginning to define the activities of the mind; relating them to our everyday experience. Actually, there exists an orderly, scientific process of mind. Once we understand this orderly process, we can take dominion of our thought. I call this Self-Direction. It is Psychogenesis at work.

LIFE IS GOVERNED BY LAW

Every part of life is governed by law. This is a universe of law and order. There are laws of physics, laws of mathematics, laws of economics, and laws that apply to human relations. These laws have always existed.

The law that we are using in the study of Psychogenesis is this: *Every thought that one consciously thinks makes an impression on the subconscious mind that will be expressed as action according to the strength and the desire contained within the thought.*

Contrast this with what is commonly believed today. Many people believe in fate. The fatalist, and there are many, believes that life unfolds according to a preordained pattern, that there is nothing he can do about it, the circumstances being entirely beyond his control. We hear people say, "Life has dealt me one blow after another." This is the remark of a fatalist who believes that the situations in his life are beyond his control, that life has the ability to deal out "blows" without his having anything to do with it. In this group we find those who say, "Why did this have to happen to me?" Obviously, such a person believes that an unkind fate, beyond his control, stepped into the picture and did something to him. Another fatalistic viewpoint is expressed in the comment, "Things just aren't going right with me anymore."

In the world of popular belief, superstition is the rule, and "Lady Luck," queen of the domain. Some of the comments heard are: "It's just my luck!" "I'm not lucky these days," "I had the good fortune to stumble on a good thing," or, "I had the ill-fortune to lose all I had." Good luck, or bad luck, it is all a misunderstanding of the law.

WITH APOLOGIES TO PERRY MASON

Sometimes it is easier to see how the mind works by observing some of the more dramatic results of our negative thinking. The following cases point up what happens when people use Self-Direction in reverse to claim for themselves that which they do not really want; things that later they consider the cruel injustices of fate. These are true stories told to me by people who came to me for help. They wanted to be rid of circumstances which they had drawn to themselves by giving the wrong orders to the subconscious mind.

THE CASE OF THE TIME-LIMITED INVENTOR

Several years ago I knew a chap who was a terrific inventor. He had brilliant ideas and put them to use. He invented many useful items. Why do I call him the "time-limited inventor"? It is because he had a bad habit that kept him from succeeding. He kept saying, "I've researched all of the great inventors and an inventor doesn't begin to be successful until he has been an inventor for twelve years." He had to go back to a paying job that took all of his time and kept him from inventing many useful items. He set up the law for himself and what a shame it was.

THE CASE OF THE COLORED HANDKERCHIEF

To continue further, we find The Case of the Colored Handkerchief. Here, the criminal was a little, harmless, colored handkerchief. The woman involved had set up a law for herself. A thousand times she said it, if she said it once, "Every time I use a colored handkerchief my nose becomes infected."

The result: the tiniest pink rosebud printed on a handker-chief would seem to cause her nose to become red and sore and swollen. Another case of the wrong use of Self-Direction.

Every thought that one consciously thinks makes an impres-sion on the subconscious mind that will be expressed as ac-tion according to the strength and the desire contained within the thought.

Actually, every time the woman used the colored handker-chief she did have a swollen nose. Was it the dye in the cloth? No. She had put a law into action.

THE CASE OF THE FRACTURED PIMPLE

A boy in our neighborhood died from blood poisoning caused by a pimple on his face. A family I knew picked this up and established a law for themselves. Every time a person in this family had a pimple on his face he became gravely concerned. The family considered that any break above the neckline was apt to be fatal. Whenever a blemish appeared, there was great concern. There was dousing with disinfec-tants, iodine, or whatever was the prevailing preparation; they rushed to the doctor and, full of fear, awaited what might well be inevitable death. You and I know that this kind of blood poisoning is comparatively rare. Hundreds of thou-sands of teenagers with skin disorders survive with little or no attention paid to skin hygiene, yet, in this family two members of the family became gravely ill with blood poison-ing due to facial skin eruptions. They had established a law for themselves and they reaped the result.

THERE IS A WAY OUT OF EVERY DIFFICULTY

How fortunate we are that there is a way out of these self-made difficulties. We do not have to sleep forever in the un-comfortable beds that we make for ourselves.

The answer lies in retraining our subconscious minds.

Since the subconscious mind is the builder of the body and its affairs, we begin by changing the orders that we have previously given it. At this point, we discover that while we may consciously affirm a new life for ourselves, unles we convince the subconscious mind of our new train of thinking, it goes right on producing for us the orders that we gave it last week, last month, or even years ago. It knows only to serve us and it does the job well. The subconscious mind is a faithful servant that continues to fill our orders until we definitely change them. The orders that it knows and follows are what we really believe about ourselves.

Have you been in the habit of thinking of yourself as lacking energy, tiring easily, being subject to every contagious disease that comes along? If you have, don't be surprised if that is your experience. The order taker and the delivery department are in complete accord. The subconscious mind is continually producing into our experience *that which it thinks we want*.

Now, we are going to learn how to redirect the subconscious mind, erasing the old negative patterns and replacing them with new affirmative ones. There is a definite technique to be followed. Self-Direction is an art well worth learning.

SELF-DIRECTION
FOR A BRIGHT NEW LIFE

This is the turning point in my life.
I am erasing the past. The future is mine to choose.
Right this moment I am making my tomorrows.
I forgive myself for all past mistakes.
I start over with a clean slate.
I choose for myself only that which I desire to experience.
I choose: (You name it: health, wealth, abundance,
           happiness, companionship, achievement—
           the subconscious mind will go to work to
           produce it for you.)
           CLAIM IT—IT'S YOURS!

IV DARE TO BE YOURSELF

> *This above all,—To thine own self be true;*
> *And it must follow, as the night the day,*
> *Thou canst not then be false to any man.*
> SHAKESPEARE, *Hamlet*

STAND on the corner of the main intersection in your city and watch the people go by . . . how tense and worried they look. This is because they are rejecting themselves. We are all prone to reject ourselves. The tendency is to think that we are being rejected by others, but that really is not the case at all. We are rejecting ourselves, and it shows in our faces.

A speech teacher was instructing his class, telling them, "Whenever you speak, always have your facial expressions harmonize with what you are talking about. If you are talking about heaven, for instance, let your eyes shine and your face radiate, and let a kind of glow come from you. Then, when you are talking about hell . . . well, just use your everyday expression." What is your everyday expression? Is it the expression of a person who does not accept himself, who thoroughly rejects himself?

THE HOUR OF SELF-ACCEPTANCE

Do you know how wonderful you are? You are the image and likeness of the Creator. You are an inlet and an outlet for the brilliance of the divine Mind. All Wisdom and Power is ably expressed through you. This is the truth about you. This is the true Self.

"You are the most vital thing in the whole Universe, as far as you are concerned. No matter where you are, what you are, how big or how little your life may be; you are, and always will be, the center of your world," wrote Frances Wilshire in her charming little book, *You.* She made it clear, however, that this is never a question of *egotism*, but of *egoism* rightly understood. Egoism, she says, is the knowledge of the real Self.

May I propose that right this very moment you launch a campaign to know and accept your real Self. Start out by declaring an hour of Self-acceptance. Each day, set aside one hour in which you accept yourself for what you really are, refusing to entertain one single thought of self-rejection. It can be done *when you know who you really are.*

> *Truth is within ourselves; it takes no rise*
> *From outward things, whate'er you may believe.*
> *There is an inmost centre in us all,*
> *Where truth abides in fullness; and to KNOW*
> *Rather consists in opening out a way*
> *Whence the imprisoned splendor may escape,*
> *Than in effecting entry for a light*
> *Supposed to be without.*
>
> Robert Browning

MAN TENDS TO UNDERRATE HIMSELF

The tendency of man is to belittle himself. He constantly rates himself in terms of comparison with how others appear to him.

What can a mere man do here on earth? He can do much. He can accomplish a great deal. He who is aware of his own true Self, the Divinity within him, can do the so-called impossible.

Man can do whatever he is able to conceive in his mind, receive in his consciousness, expect with assurance, and accept in actual experience. The Universe does not set limitations. *We set them by our own belief about ourselves.*

DISCOVERING THE TRUE SELF

If a person is trying to find himself, where did he lose himself? Did he ever know himself to begin with?

I remember a man telling me that each person was trying to find himself and that only the mature person succeeded. He said that the very seeking was the first step toward maturity.

One time a V.I.P. (very important person), sitting across my desk from me, remarked, "My big problem is to find myself!" I looked at him in a quizzical way and asked, "Well, if you could find yourself, what would you like to find?"

He looked rather astonished. He said nothing for a few moments, then he slowly told me what he was really thinking: "Well, it's very simple. I'd like to be like John Fitzgerald . . . he's the president of his company . . . he's the president of his service club . . . he's in civic activities . . . he's very prosperous . . . people look up to him . . . he's very important."

"But," I replied, "you are not trying to find *yourself!* You're trying to find John Fitzgerald! He is he and you are you. Each one is unique, expressing life in his own particular way. If you were the same, you would cancel each other out. The words 'finding yourself' are confusing. You have never lost yourself. No, it's not a matter of finding *yourself,* but of uncovering the *true Self* that is already there. Where? Not apart from you. Not *out there.*

"We are really trying to uncover the perfect, divine Self that is right here, right within each one of us. It's just as though we were uncovering buried treasure. We must get rid of all of the debris of negative thinking, the pile of fearful thoughts we have entertained over the years, thoughts that have obscured the true Self."

"I think I see what you're driving at," the man across from me said. "What are some of those negative or fearful thoughts that you mentioned?"

"Their names are legion," I replied. "Here are a few: self-ishness, pride, vanity, self-righteousness, jealousy, self-pity, resentment, deceit, self-condemnation, envy, distrust, criticism, hate, insecurity, despair, hostility—on and on and on."

"I see! Yes! I see!" he exclaimed. "I have been rejecting my real Self while trying to find a self that did not exist for me. Jesus knew what he was talking about when he told us to seek the Kingdom of God right within us and that all else would be added."

IT'S THREE TO ONE YOU CAN

Margaret Blair Johnson in an article in *Guideposts* magazine tells a story of how she nearly left the ministry within a short time after she had begun. She was sent to upper New York State to take over a parish in which there were three widely separated churches to be served by one minister. She had to make the rounds of these three churches every Sunday. Her husband was overseas in the service. She had two babies. Many things seemed to go wrong, but the big blow came one Saturday night. It was below zero outside, snow was falling. It was near midnight when, of all things, the oil heater exploded. She lived in a remote area. A neighbor came over and put the fire out, but she decided that this was it! She picked up the phone and, even though it was the middle of the night, she got through to the district superintendent of her denomination. She could hear the telltale sound of other phones on her party line being picked up . . . neighbors listening in . . . but she did not care. She poured out the whole story to him and then told him, "Well, I've had it. You'd

better get somebody else up here right away. I can't go on!
I can't go on!"

The next morning she found an envelope at her front door
and in it was an unsigned letter which simply said, "It's three
to one you can." The writer then quoted from the letter that
Paul wrote to Timothy, and set it up this way:

> For God hath not given us the spirit of fear;
> but of power,
> and of love,
> and of a sound mind.

Yes, she saw that fear was outnumbered three to one and
she began to laugh, to laugh at herself for letting herself be
caught up in this foolish situation of thinking that she could
not go on. All of a sudden, she knew she could go on. Life
was with her, not against her. She did continue on, writing
several books and many articles, while conducting a highly
successful ministry. Those six words were the turning point:
It's three to one you can.

So often we are faced with situations where we wonder if
we can go on, but it's three to one we can, because all of life
is with us—nothing is against us. That which seems to be
against us is that which we build up ourselves. There is no
power in Life that is in any way opposing the real Self.

YOU ARE NEVER ALONE

In your daily hour of Self-acceptance, it is good to know
that you are not alone, that within you is the Wholeness of
Life. *The ground upon which you stand is holy ground.* All
of the creativity, the power and wonder of Life lives through
you, giving you all that you need to fulfill your desires and
expectations.

Fear has many children; envy, hate, resentment, and all the
negative thinking mentioned before are the children of fear.
Shall we let fear rule us? We don't need to. God did not give

us fear. We adopted all of those children and they are the bane of our existence. God has given us love and *perfect Love casteth out fear*. What is this perfect Love that casts out fear? Loving the Self is a realization that there is that within which is able to do all things through us, for us. It is a realization that the Power within is able to do all things through us. That which created us is the activity of divine Love. Love did not create us and put us in a vacuum, or into a hostile atmosphere. Love did not create us and put us into impossible situations.

That which created us loves us, and this Love is unconditioned by circumstances. It is not conditioned by who we are, where we live, or our position in life. It is not conditioned by any person, place, thing, or circumstance. Unconditioned Love lives through us and will cast out fear. Furthermore, unconditioned Love is everywhere present. Therefore, wherever we go, we find Love. We can go to foreign lands and we will find Love expressed through people in their own particular way. God gave us Himself to individualize, to particularize, and to personalize. Each one of us expresses God at his own point of awareness.

IMITATION IS SUICIDE

When one rejects himself, he is rejecting Life. When one condemns himself, he condemns Life. Emerson said that imitation is suicide. One does not have to imitate another to be complete and fulfilled. Each one must trust the Wisdom, the Power, and the Love being expressed through him. We all draw from the same Source. We may make mistakes, but, so what! What is a mistake but someone's opinion of how something should have been done? Who knows? Be yourself and you cannot make mistakes. You will still be yourself. There is an old proverb: *The only people who never make mistakes are those who never do anything*. What are mistakes but find-

ing ways and means of doing something better the next time?
Sometimes they seem costly, but nothing can really be costly.
You can't lose anything. You are from an Infinite Source and
nothing can be taken from the Infinite. Just back up and try
again.

WHAT IS YOUR DOMINANT DESIRE?

What would you like to do, *really* like to do, if you knew
that you could choose your course; if you knew that it was
impossible for you to fail? Are you absolutely satisfied with
your life as it is today, or would you like to alter it according
to your heart's desire? Do you believe that you are a pawn in
the hand of fate? This is not the truth. You are the one who
calls the shots. You are a dictator in an absolute domain. It
is impossible for you to fail. You can have your heart's desire.
You can chart your course and realize your goals if you understand how to do it. The key is Self-Direction. It must all
start with *you*.

> There is one mind common to all individual men. Every man
> is an inlet to the same and to all of the same. He that is once
> admitted to the right of reason is a freeman of the whole estate.
> What Plato has thought, he may feel; what has at any time
> befallen any man, he can understand. Who hath access to this
> universal mind is a party to all that is or can be done; for this
> is the only and sovereign agent . . . of this Universal Mind each
> individual is one more incarnation.[1]

Like fish in the sea we move about in the infinite sea of
Mind. It is around us and passes through us. It provides for
our every need. What Plato has thought, we may think; but
just as the sea pays no attention to what the fish receives from

[1] Ralph Waldo Emerson, "History," *Essays*, (Boston and New York: Hough-
ton Mifflin Co., 1881).

its infinite resources, so the Universal Mind pays no heed to what each one of us may choose to draw from it.

Like Abraham of old, we are told: *For all the land which thou seest, to thee will I give it.*[2]

"The creative Force of the universe is working through you," wrote Robert Collier. "You can be as great an outlet for it as anyone who has ever lived. You have only to provide the mold in which it is to take shape, and that mold is formed by your thoughts. What is your dominant desire? What do you want most? Believe in it and you can have it. Make it your dominating thought, magnetize your mind with it, and you will draw to you everything you need for its accomplishment."[3]

DARE TO BE YOURSELF

I know a man who is worth over a million dollars. To meet him you would think that he had a very limited income. He owns two suits of clothes, two shirts, and probably two pair of socks. He is one of the most generous men I have ever known. He thinks nothing of giving $100,000 to promote an idea or a cause, yet he is loathe to spend a penny on himself. To travel first-class could seem to him rank extravagance. As far as he is concerned a person is a fool to spend money on any luxury, and yet he could have the best, for he could not spend the money that he has in this lifetime. To him, it is better to use it, or leave it, to promote a cause that is dear to his heart. He would not change his life. It is the life that he has chosen.

It was Henry David Thoreau, himself a rugged individualist, who wrote that every man should walk to the drumbeat that he hears. Each one of us has his own drummer boy, and to walk to the beat of another's drum is to be out of step with life.

[2] Genesis 13:15.
[3] Robert Collier, *The Law of the Higher Potential*, (Tarrytown, N.Y.: Robert Collier Publishing, Inc., 1947).

George Chapman wrote:

> Who to himself is law no law does need,
> Offends no law, and is a king indeed.

The man I mentioned, who is frugal with himself and generous with others, is walking to the drumbeat that he hears. Too many people today try to keep up with the drumbeat of the masses. They suffer nervous exhaustion and nervous breakdowns, live on pep pills and tranquilizers because they are trying to keep up with what they think people expect of them, instead of listening to their own inner Guidance.

The great Universal Mind, individualized in us, gives us the choice. We can be daring and do the things that we would like to do, or be safe and do the things that other people would like to have us do. Each one specializes the Mind according to his belief about himself. Our consciousness is *what we believe about ourselves* and our experience here on earth. *As thou has believed, so be it done unto you*, said the Master Teacher.

DARE TO CHOOSE YOUR THOUGHTS AND
PROTECT THEM WELL

In his book *Think and Grow Rich* Napoleon Hill writes:

You have absolute control over but one thing, and that is your thoughts. This is the most significant and inspiring of all facts known to man! It reflects man's divine nature. This divine prerogative is the sole means by which you may control your own destiny. If you fail to control your own mind, you may be sure you will control nothing else. If you must be careless with your possessions, let it be in connection with material things. Your mind is your spiritual estate! Protect and use it with the care to which divine royalty is entitled. You were given a willpower for this purpose.[4]

4 Napoleon Hill, *Think and Grow Rich*, (New York: Fawcett World Library, 1961).

Too many people think that they can storm the gates of heaven without taking dominion over their own lives. Before we can enter into our divine heritage, which the Bible refers to as the kingdom of heaven within, we must take dominion over our own thoughts. Taking a short cut to heaven just doesn't work. We can't sneak in through the back door, or climb over the fence, because once we got there we would find that we'd left behind so much unfinished business that we'd have to go right back and tend to it.

> Enter ye in at the strait gate: for wide is the gate, and broad is the way, that leadeth to destruction, and many there be which go in thereat:
> Because strait is the gate, and narrow is the way, which leadeth unto life, and few there be that find it.

To enter by the straight and narrow way is to realize that we are living in a universe of law and order. It has been said, *order is the first rule of heaven.* To get our lives in order we must take dominion of our thoughts. This is not always easy. First, it is necessary to choose the kind of thoughts that we would like to see taking form in our experience. Second, we must strive to protect our thoughts against the infiltration of race thinking. Third, we must set about to erase old thought patterns that might tend to impinge upon our new thinking. To this end we must learn Self-Direction.

WHAT IS THIS THING CALLED MIND?

We have said that we dwell in a sea of Mind. In it we *live and move and have our being.* When we talk about the brain, we are not talking about the Mind. To say that a person is "quite a brain" is a misnomer. The brain is the instrument of the mind for our use. It tunes in on the sea of Mind very much like a radio tunes in on the sea of sound waves. Mind is universal, everywhere present. Like the kingdom of heaven within, it is not *lo here,* or *lo there.* It is not confined to any one area or any one person. Thinking, then, *is our use of Mind at our point of awareness.*

I like what a famous doctor had to say about it:

The brain does not secrete thought as the liver secretes bile.

The Mind is not in the brain, nor is the Mind anywhere in the universe of space. Space, like time, is but man's concept of the universe and depends upon two points that man selects. Space is measurable only according to man's human judgement. It is purely relative. Mind is universal. It has no limitation. Nothing can encompass Mind. The realm of Mind is not confined to the human skull. Quantity of brain cells has nothing to do with it. Gray matter has nothing to do with it. It is our use of Mind that counts. Thus, a person who is able to open his mind to receive ideas from the Universal Storehouse is a more effective thinker than the person who depends entirely upon his educational qualifications.

One of the saddest things today is the way some people are given preference over others simply because they are college graduates. Many times the person who is not a college graduate may have more ability, more creativity, more useful information in his field than the person who has the college degree. It is said of many people that when they wrap up their college diploma they wrap up their brains with it. To be sure, there are those who wrap up their initiative and their feeling of accomplishment and put it away at that time.

There is one Mind common to all men, the creative Mind of the Universe. Emerson called it the Over-Soul. Jesus called it Father. Paul Brunton, a great student of the Eastern religions, called it the Over-Self. Dr. Pitirim Sorokin, the great sociologist, calls it the Supra-Conscious Mind. Others have called it the Super-Conscious Mind or God.

THE TWO ASPECTS OF MIND

While there is one Mind common to all men, there are two aspects of that Mind, two functions or uses of it. They are called conscious mind and subconscious mind. Sometimes the subconscious mind is spoken of as the unconscious mind and sometimes the subjective mind. I prefer to call it the subconscious mind. The conscious mind is your use of Mind through conscious awareness. It is that mind which you think of as your awake mind. You use it during your waking hours. The subconscious mind is that part of your mind of which you are not aware. It has been likened to the nine-tenths of an iceberg beneath the level of the sea. Your conscious use of the Mind is only a small fraction of the whole Mind. When I say *your* mind and *my* mind, remember that I am only speaking of our use of the Universal or Great Mind. We each identify with a certain point of use of Mind and therein lies our individuality.

You use the conscious mind only during the hours that you are awake, but your subconscious use of Mind goes right on working for you twenty-four hours a day. As it is so beautifully expressed in the Psalms, *He that keepeth Israel neither slumbers nor sleeps.*

The subconscious mind operates your body functions. You may eat a late dinner and go peacefully to sleep, never giving a thought to the intricate process of digesting your food that goes right on during your sleep. The subconscious mind knows how to run our bodies if we will leave it alone. It is not necessary to give the body one thing to step it up and another thing to slow it down. For those who live right, it is not necessary to take a single thought about the working of the organs and cells of the body. Those who do simply do not trust the subconscious mind. Your subconscious mind knows how to operate your body and how to make it function perfectly. Infinite Intelligence is at work in the tiniest measure of life, the atom. Only our fears and anxieties, our various kinds of stress, get in the way. The subconscious mind is not only the keeper of the body, but the builder of the body and the builder of our lives and affairs.

WE CAN HAVE WHAT WE WANT

We understand so little about the working out of life. For instance, we take electricity for granted. We only know that if we plug into the circuit, we can bring a light into the room, or use our toaster or coffee maker. We have been warned how not to use it, but we do not know why or what happens. I know very little about electricity, but I do know a few things. I would not think of taking an electrical connection in my hand and getting into a tub filled with water because I know that if I did I would make short shrift of myself— that is, my life here on earth. Nor would I go around touching live wires. I know that I would get a shock.

What most of us don't realize is that it is even more dangerous to resist life, to hate and condemn other persons, or to strive and struggle and build up strees in our minds. Once we understand, even a little bit, about the working of the subconscious mind, we realize how important it is to get the hindrances out of the way of its perfect functioning. There is nothing on earth quite so important as to purge our subconscious thinking of these little foxes that spoil the vines. An understanding of the subconscious mind, at our point of use, is the most important thing that we can ever learn. The Universal Subconscious Mind is so wise, all-knowing, and sensitive, that It will respond to our every request, honor our every demand. It will carry out every idea or suggestion that we give it. Why, then, are we ever unhappy or lacking in anything that our hearts desire?

TAKING DOMINION

There is only one point where we can take dominion of our lives and that is at our point of use of the conscious mind. Once we have thought a thought it goes to work, just as a seed planted in the ground starts producing a plant that will ultimately bear fruit. As long as the seed is left in the ground under proper conditions it knows only to reproduce after its kind. It is the conscious mind that does the directing. Out of it come the thought seeds that start the growth cycle. We have the choice; it is up to us, these seeds we will plant. A person who doesn't like cucumbers is a fool to plant cucumbers in his garden. In the same way, unless we take dominion in our thought garden, we are going to cause the subconscious mind to work through us to our own detriment. It does not judge any more than the soil judges the seed that is planted. In fact, it has been called the *soil of the mind*. It knows only to respond to the seed thoughts that are given it. Disease and disorder of every kind result from our own failure to understand the working of the subconscious mind so that we may use it wisely in our lives.

It is the conscious mind that does the directing. Here we choose the kind of thoughts that will provide the mold for the kind of experiences that we would like. As we study Self-Direction we learn the proper way to use and direct the subconscious mind. The conscious mind selects the way in which we shall relate ourselves to life. It selects our various avenues of expression. It is the center of choice. It does the planning. The conscious mind gives orders to the subconscious mind which in turn acts upon them. As the Bible says, *it moves upon the face of the deep.* The power rests with the conscious mind which selects, chooses, reasons, projects, and plans. The subconscious mind will always produce the outward manifestation that is agreed upon. If we don't like what is being produced, where should we turn? It is only the order giver who can rescind the order and start a new chain of creative activity. Self-Direction is taking dominion of the little wayward self. It is choosing the kind of thoughts we will think, knowing that the thoughts are the orders that we give the Universal Subconscious Mind. Mind goes to work for us, drawing upon the Whole to produce exactly what we have ordered. We can have what we want depending upon our choices. It is therefore highly desirable that we make wise choices.

SELF-DIRECTION

I am now opening my mind to receive ideas. I know that I have available to me a vast storehouse of knowledge, an infinite array of creative ideas, ideas that have never been tried before. At my point of use of the One Mind, I know intuitively all that I need to know. I am guided and directed to make wise choices, choices that will result in right activity in my life and affairs. I now still the mind of all fear and anxiety. I trust the infinite Intelligence within me to guide and direct me into channels of creative activity. In quietness and confidence I receive my strength. I am open and receptive to ideas and inspiration that will multiply my good in wondrous ways.

And so it is.

V FIVE STEPS TO
ACHIEVING YOUR GOALS

Do the thing and you will have the power.
RALPH WALDO EMERSON

THE other day a young man telephoned me from Winnipeg, Canada. He had just read a book of mine and wanted to know if he could come down to see me. Three days later he was sitting in my study. As we discussed my radio programs, he asked me, "What are your goals?" I must confess that momentarily I was stumped. Caught up in the daily activity of script writing, lecturing, and a heavy correspondence, I realized that I had lost sight of my real goals. I had at one time set down goals in my journal, but of late they had become submerged in the day-to-day effort to sustain the work at hand. They had become dim in my mind. His remark brought me up short. For the moment, I had actually forgotten my goals. I saw that I had been losing sight of them because of what seemed to be realistic thinking, but was really thinking that had become limited. Here was I, a person who not only believed in goal setting and taught others that they were only limited by the goals they set, but forgetting my own goals. I had become bogged down in detail. His remark caused me to turn again to the dream that I had set down in my journal.

This young man who caused me to reexamine my own goals had already achieved a few of his own. At thirty-eight he had sold his business for over a million dollars and was ready to retire from the commercial world. Now, he was offering to dedicate his time and considerable ability to helping me realize my goals. His next remark inspired this chapter. He said, "The thing we've got to do is set up the goals, *no matter how impossible they may seem at this moment,* and then start moving toward them."

THE FIVE STEPS

I am going to give you five steps that start with belief and end with manifestation. They are as practical as the teaching of one of the outstanding goal setters of all time who said, *What things soever ye desire, when ye pray, believe that ye receive them and ye shall have them.*[1] It is a matter of: *act as though I am, and I will be.*

1. Set up for yourself the ideal mental image.
2. Faith without works is dead.
3. Keep your own counsel.
4. Be flexible; revise the plan when necessary.
5. Keep your eye on the finished picture; don't stop half-way.

SET UP FOR YOURSELF THE IDEAL MENTAL IMAGE

The key to goal setting is again: *that which you can conceive of, believe in, and confidently expect for yourself must necessarily become your experience.* It is important that the goal relate to the person in such a way that he can finally accept it for himself. Almost no goal is impossible of attainment if you can accept it as being within the realm of possibility. An example of this is Demosthenes who had a bad speech impediment, stammered and stuttered. Who would have thought that he could become a great orator? Yet, he persevered. The story is that he put pebbles in his mouth and made himself talk around them. Finally, he overcame his

[1] Mark 11:24.

speech impediment and achieved his goal. He became a great orator.

Belief is the first step; belief in yourself and the Power within you. The apostle Paul called this *the evidence of things unseen.* Dramatize yourself in your mind's eye as doing what seems to you as the ideal thing, living the ideal life, being the ideal person. The self-image that you set determines how you relate to your goal.

If you set the goal of writing a book, you must create, within yourself, the image of being a writer. If a person wants to be a great trial lawyer he must create for himself the image of being a lawyer. He could hardly be a person who constantly maintained that he could not speak before a crowd.

Once a young man came to me and asked me to help him attain the goal of being a successful touring golfer. He had been reading in the paper about how much money they made. I asked him, "What kind of a game do you shoot?" He said, "I don't know. I don't play golf."

Don't be grim about your goals. Be joyful about your new image. Life responds to the light treatment, not the heavy drama. Be as happy about your goal as if it was already in your grasp. It is, really. Once you have accepted it, nothing can keep it from you. Keep telling yourself: "I have accepted this."

Emile Zola, in his autobiography, tells of his three goals. They were: 1. To have a child. 2. To write a book. 3. To plant a tree. He wrote numerous books; had children; and eventually planted many trees on his estate. His goals pertained to the continuity of life. He felt that his *raison d'etre* was to continue life. The books left something to posterity on the mental level, the tree, the physical level, and the children on the spiritual level.

Mahatma Ghandi set for himself a fantastic goal. Who could have imagined that this unimposing little man who seemed physically incapable of accomplishing much, would be the instrument for freeing India from the powerful British Empire?

BE CAREFUL NOT TO LIMIT YOUR GOALS

Only you can judge your goals and you should beware of your judgment for more than likely you will limit yourself. Every year parents or grandparents graduate from college and start new careers. The father of a friend of mine started practicing law at sixty-five and became very successful. He didn't start studying law until he was sixty-one when many people would have said it was too late to start over. Yet, his legal practice continued for twenty years during which time he made quite a name for himself. Grandma Moses started painting at seventy-eight and became world famous as an artist by the time she was ninety—to the surprise of her family and everyone else. Many people who were farsighted enough to buy her paintings are glad today they did! How fortunate that this little lady didn't think that it was too late to start a new career at seventy-eight.

Both Herbert Hoover and his son, Herbert Hoover, Jr., set lofty goals for themselves and attained them. Herbert Hoover, Sr. set for himself this goal: He wanted to make enough money by the time he was forty to devote the rest of his life to public service. He graduated from Stanford University with a degree in geology. Here was a man who we would say today "had all the strikes against him." His parents both died when he was a young child; he was farmed out to relatives and had to earn his entire way through college. When he graduated, in the first graduating class at Stanford, he went to work—not as a geologist or mining engineer expert, but as a day laborer in a California mine. He soon graduated from this rough work and, as we all know, made a name for himself in mining engineering. Before he reached forty he had become a consultant for a score of mining companies and had offices in San Francisco, New York, and London. Now, a multimillionaire while still a young man, he was ready to help mankind and this he did with spectacular success. After World War I broke out he was called upon to distribute food to the starving nations. Throughout the war he sent into occupied Belgium and France some five million tons of food and clothing with a market value of $1 billion accomplishing this huge task in the face of great and continuing diplomatic and practical difficulties. This success brought him world fame. It would take volumes to list his other accomplishments in his dedicated service to mankind. We know him best as the thirty-first president of the United States.

Obviously, Herbert Hoover, Jr. set for himself a similar goal. He attained his goal through oil exploration, the gold of his day, and retired at forty to give his life to public service.

Man's propensity is to sell himself short, to underestimate his own abilities, his own potential. Sometimes, we need to have our goals set by someone else who is more aware of what we can accomplish. An example of this is the sales manager who sets such high goals for his men that they have to continually strive to make the quotas.

A friend of mine, a very successful business consultant, told me a story the other day about one of his clients, an insurance brokerage firm. This firm had done $700,000 worth of business during the past year. My friend told them, "Next year you're going to do $1,300,000." The response was, "You must be crazy! That's nearly double what we did this year." My friend had taken into consideration potentials that they had not even thought about. He was serious in making this forecast. The next year this insurance brokerage firm not only attained the forecast but exceeded it by several thousand dollars. *Ah, but a man's reach must exceed his grasp.*[2] Goal setting begins in mind. It is a matter of Self-Direction.

[2] Robert Browning, "Andrea del Sarto."

FAITH WITHOUT WORKS IS DEAD

This is the department of works. Do something about your goals. Move forward; take the steps. To set goals and take no action on them is self-defeating. Faith without works is not only dead but completely unproductive. If we don't act upon our faith, it becomes mere daydreaming. *By work is faith made perfect.*

Many people talk about a goal without ever intending to do a thing about it. Often there is some block that prevents them from moving in the direction of their goal—the fear of failure, the fear of being ridiculed, the fear of hurting someone else, or, the fear of what others may think.

A WOMAN WHO DARED TO ACT UPON HER FAITH

Now I am going to tell you a story by way of illustration. It is about a woman who dared to act upon her faith. I think she had gotten to the point, after many years of daydreaming, that she was just plain tired of the futility of it all. She had never been married, although she had wanted to be married for many years. Maybe it was because her mother was living with her and she didn't want to hurt Mother's feelings. The man that she wanted to marry lived on one of the Hawaiian Islands in a beautiful home overlooking a bay. He had a good income and, being a very creative person, lived a good life. His great dream was to have this woman be his wife. This was the story that the woman laid before me.

When she had finished, I said, "You came to me for help, but obviously, you aren't prepared to do a thing about it."

"What do you mean?" she asked.

I said, "Well, suppose your inner guidance is to go to this man and marry him. You love each other and all of Life desires your happiness, but would you do what you were guided to do? At present, you are too close to Mother. You wouldn't do anything about it. You wouldn't take steps to bring it to pass."

She said, "Yes, I see what you mean. There's no need to accept the idea unless I am willing to do something about it. I will do something about it." We had a wonderful, affirmative prayer of acceptance together, which, in my work, I call treatment.

Our friend went home and started packing. The mother began to get worried and asked her what she was going to do. She told her mother she was going to Hawaii to marry the man she had wanted to marry for so many years. Well, it all worked out. Mother didn't have that heart attack she had threatened daughter with, after all. She even found that she liked living alone. The couple were married and lived happily ever after. Formerly, the woman had put the idea into mind, but wasn't doing anything about it. You have to be willing to take the human footsteps. This, however, is far different from starting on the outside and trying to make things happen by manipulating life.

We start by creating the ideal mental image in faith, knowing the Power must be used in love, and then act upon the Guidance as we receive it. We go within to get our inspiration, and then live it in expression.

KEEP YOUR OWN COUNSEL

Keep the mental image to yourself. Do the thing and let the results speak for themselves. Tell no one.

So often, we let off steam when we talk to others and the power is gone. Perhaps you are very enthusiastic about a certain idea, your inspiration at that point is complete with all of the power and enthusiasm necessary to bring it into manifestation. You tell your dream to another and somehow it doesn't fit into his line of thinking at all. He begins to throw cold water on it. He can't see how it is feasible at all. Before he is through, all of the air has been let out of your sails, there isn't anything left.

Continue with your mental image, taking the necessary human footsteps as they are given to you by your Guidance within. Keep the faith, but don't tell anyone about it, not even your nearest or dearest. Let the results speak for themselves. Yes, there are times when other people may have to be brought into the experience—when it becomes a joint enterprise. You can still keep your mental image to yourself in the sense that you are not going to let their applause or derision have any effect on you. You may have to expose your idea; but, when you do, expose it in the light of Truth, with a feeling of assurance because you believe in it. Don't let yourself be swayed one way or another by the response. Remember, some of the best books have been rejected by many publishers. You cannot afford to let yourself get caught up in someone else's negation.

BE FLEXIBLE; REVISE THE PLAN WHEN NECESSARY

A goal must be something that we really want to attain. As we grow in understanding we may want to change our goals or adapt them to our present thinking. The goal of a tree is to stand upright, but it is important that it be able to bend with the wind. If we set a rigid goal, it may be attainable, but it may break us in the process.

Sometimes our goals are realized in unexpected ways. Take, for instance, a man I once knew who dreamed of owning a horse ranch. He thought that it was necessary to first make a lot of money in order to afford his dream. He labored in the business world for many years attaining great success. Eventually, he felt that he was rich enough to have the long desired horse ranch. Much to his surprise he found that horse breeding was a very lucrative business. He could have been enjoying his real goal all along without going through the long and frustrating years in the business world.

Contrast him with another man I knew who longed to have an avocado orchard. He began studying about avocados, learning about horticulture and all of the things that go to make up the life of an avocado grower. While still engaged in his original business he bought acreage in avocado country and set out a few trees. Within a year or so he was out of the garage business and well on the way to becoming one of the most successful avocado growers in the business.

Consider the story of Dr. James Turpin, founder of Project Concern. Jim first set a goal of being a good doctor and a community leader. By the time he was in his early thirties he was one of the leading doctors in his city and was on the city council. His change of goals came about in an interesting way. He was asked to give one afternoon a week to serve as the volunteer physician at a free medical clinic in Mexico. He told me that after he had done this work for several weeks he found that he was looking forward to Thursday afternoons as being the high spot in the week. Everything else paled by comparison. After I went with him to the Casa de Todas clinic one week, I knew what he meant. This rewarding work caused him to change his goal. His new goal was to establish free medical clinics all over the world in those places where medical help was unavailable. Out of this came Project Concern with clinics in numerous places such as Hong Kong, South Viet Nam, and Mexico.

**KEEP YOUR EYE ON THE FINISHED PICTURE;
DON'T STOP HALFWAY**

If you keep your attention on the goal, your subconscious mind will fill in the details. It will actually bring into your experience the people who are needed to help you, the right opportunities and situations favorable to its successful conclusion. Your job is to develop for yourself a consciousness of actually experiencing the goal you would like to realize.

As God said to Abraham, *All of the land which thou seest, to thee will I give it; but go ye in and possess the land.*[3]

Mentally finish the dream and then complete it in the outer. We don't have to outline all the details, but we do have to go in and possess the land (consciousness). Imagine yourself as happily married, successful in business, healthy and active, loved and beloved by all—whatever the need may be. Surround yourself mentally with the very climate of the experience. Then, as Emerson said, "Do the thing and you will have the power."

One job finished is worth fifty half finished. Mentally finish it *in mind* and then take steps to finish it outwardly.

One time a real estate man came to see me. He seemed to have plenty of activity in his business, but none of it ever completely materialized. He would get a sale into escrow and then something would happen whereby the deal would fall through, not once, but over and over. It was just unbelievable until one analyzed his thinking. As we talked, it developed that one of the things he kept saying again and again, until it had become a pattern with him, was, "Well, I'll get that deal into escrow." It was all right as far as it went. He had to revise his mental image of a real estate deal. The real estate transaction is completed when the money is distributed and the property is taken over by the new owner. He set this into mind and from that time on completed his sales. As the mental image was changed, the new experience followed. So many times we have a mental image up to a point, but not all the way.

We must think of our project, whatever it is, as finished and complete, and then take the steps that are presented, to realize it in our experience. Otherwise, we ask amiss; like the person who prays night and day for the healing of a loved one, all the time making plans for the funeral; or one who prays beautiful prayers for success and constantly visualizes himself

[3] Genesis 13:15.

going through bankruptcy. It is *done unto you as you believe.* The subjective side of Life, the Law, acts upon our prayers at their face value and gives us that which we are willing to receive out of Life.

TAKE INVENTORY OF YOUR GOALS

Now and then, take a mental inventory of your goals. Are you sure you are moving in the direction of what you really want out of life? Are you one who thinks he would like to be prosperous but spends all of his time thinking about what is lacking? Do you feel impoverished every time you pay a bill? Do you long for companionship, but think of yourself as desolate and alone? *A man is the sum total of what he thinks about all day long.*

If you are spending all of your time thinking about what you *don't want to experience* you are like a football player who runs in the wrong direction. One of the most remembered plays of football took place in a Rose Bowl game in which one of the players ran toward the wrong goal line. I don't remember who won the game, what teams were playing, or what year it was, but I do remember that he was tackled by one of his own teammates. How often we give emphasis in our thinking to the times we run toward the wrong goal line—the failures—the stock market losses—the mistakes we make! Our demonstrations of good come along so easily that we tend to take them for granted, but how we dramatize our failures! This is running toward the wrong goal line. Yes, we are all guilty at one time or another of running toward the wrong goal. Every negative thought we entertain is a step in the wrong direction.

SELF-DIRECTION

1. Write down your goals.
2. Evaluate your goals carefully. Are they goals you would really like to experience?
3. Mentally accept your goals.
4. Create the mental image of yourself living in the midst of your goals.
5. Never dwell on the opposite of your goals. Always keep the eye single.
6. Accept your goals daily; take the steps that are presented to you and you will attain your goals.

VI TAPPING THE SOURCE OF UNLIMITED IDEAS

The thoughts that come often unsought, and, as it were, drop into the mind, are commonly the most valuable of any we have, and therefore should be secured, because they seldom return again.

JOHN LOCKE

DEEP within each one of us is the Wisdom of the ages. Hidden within is an infinite Source of creative ideas that can never be exhausted. While men search upon the surface of life for the ideas that they need, frantically turning the pages of books or researching the minds of other people, there exists at the center of each one's being the very idea that would be perfect for the need. Inspiration beyond anything man has dared to believe existed, is right where he is.

WHERE DO IDEAS COME FROM?

Why do large corporations pay top salaries to idea men who, by average standards, seem to do nothing but put their feet up on a desk and relax? It is because these men provide the ideas upon which the entire organization prospers. Where do ideas come from? Where do musicians, authors, scientists, and inventors get their ideas? How is it possible for a composer to hear in his mind an entire symphony as if it had already been produced, yet it is entirely new to him? Why is it that some people are more creative than others?

The answer is that every truly creative person has learned to rely upon the unseen Source of all ideas, the Universal Subconscious Mind with which he has direct contact. The tool he uses is intuition. Intuition has been called *direct knowing, divine guidance, illumination, ideas, and hunches.* When ideas well up from deep within us, ideas that seemingly come out of nowhere, they come through intuition.

My favorite definition of intuition is *knowledge based upon insight or spiritual perception rather than on reasoning.*

Intuition can be an immediate answer to prayer in time of need. It is the *still, small voice* of the Bible. It is the idea that comes unannounced after you have given up the whole project as a loss. Intuition does not arise deliberately, but spontaneously; not voluntarily, but involuntarily.[1] It can never be coerced. It is like an unexpected voice that comes at the precise moment when it is needed. Sometimes it bids us renounce what we have been doing; sometimes it bids us take cheer; sometimes it brings us a sudden alteration of outlook, judgment, or decision. It is the most valuable thing in our lives, if we will heed it. The truly successful man or woman is the one who has learned to listen to the voice of intuition and follow its guidance.

GREAT MEN OF ALL TIME DEPEND UPON INTUITION

John K. Williams in his splendid book *The Wisdom of Your Subconscious Mind,*[2] writes, "It is now an accepted datum in psychology that the conscious mind is just the "emergent apex," the top level of an enormous and sustaining subconscious. Research has shown that the ability to bring into action this deeper area of the mind determines the suc-

[1] Paul Brunton, *The Wisdom of the Overself,* (New York: E. P. Dutton & Co., Inc., 1943).
[2] John K. Williams, *The Wisdom of Your Subconscious Mind* (Englewood Cliffs, N.J.: Prentice-Hall, Inc., 1964).

cess of every creative worker—scientist, author, musician, inventor, or business leader."

He says that "from the time of Socrates, the founder of ethical science, to the inventive genius of Edison, Ford, Marconi, Westinghouse, Einstein, and Kettering, this little understood and unrecognized area of mental activity has delivered the insight and know-how for almost every great achievement which makes possible and sustains modern civilization as we know it."

Dr. Pitirim A. Sorokin, Director of the Research Center in Creative Altruism at Harvard University, refers to the Source of intuition as the supraconscious—another name for infinite Intelligence: God. He writes:

> The supraconscious seems to be the fountainhead of the greatest achievements and discoveries in all fields of human creative activity: science, religion, philosophy, technology, ethics, law, the fine arts, economics, and politics. Without its genius and operation, through merely conscious and unconscious activities, only mediocre achievements are possible; never the greatest. A professor of English or of musical composition may know excellently all the rational rules and techniques entering into the composition of a literary or musical masterpiece; and yet, if he is devoid of the supraconscious genius, he never can become even a remote relative of the Shakespeares and Chaucers, the Bachs and Beethovens. The same is true of a professor of scientific method: if he is not graced by the supraconscious, he has no chance to become a Galileo or Newton, Plato or Kant. In this sense, the supraconscious is the highest creative energy known.

> The supraconscious creates and discovers through *supraconscious intuition*. It is different from all sensory intuitions—perception, observation—and from logical, mathematical, and syllogistic reasoning. In contrast to senses and reason, intuitional inspiration or cognition comes as a momentary flash, different from a patient sensory observation or mathematical, logical analysis. The time, moment, and the circumstances of this flash

can hardly be foreseen, predicted, or voluntarily produced. The flash often occurs in the least expected moment and conditions.[3]

HOW INTUITION "COMES THROUGH" TO MAN

Intuition in its highest sense is sublime inspiration which comes through to us when we are able to get the little, human self out of the way. As Sirokin puts it: "It transcends ego entirely and unconditionally."

It must have been in a flash of divine intuition that Jesus said, *Of myself I do nothing, the Father within doeth the works.* It was Browning's "inner splendor," St. Theresa's "not me, but God working through me." Every mystic knew that the little self must die before the divine Self could come through in all its glory.

> *For God speaketh once, yea twice, yet man perceiveth it not. In a dream, in a vision of the night, when deep sleep falleth upon men, in slumberings upon the bed; then he openeth the ears of men, and sealeth their instruction.*
>
> Job 33:14-16.

It was in deep sleep, in a dream, a vision of the night, that Elias Howe, over a hundred years ago, received the idea that made the modern sewing machine possible. For weeks he had worked on his invention. It worked except for one thing. He could not figure out how to thread the needle and still hold the upper end in the machine. He could not seem to perfect it. One night, having worked far into the night, he fell exhausted into bed. He dreamed that he had been captured by cannibals who told him that he had to perfect the sewing machine within twenty-four hours or be eaten. Around and around him the cannibals marched. And then he saw that the spear held by the cannibal chief had a hole in the point. He awakened in a cold sweat with the answer to his problem!

[3] Pitirim A. Sorokin, *The Ways and Powers of Love*, (Boston: Beacon Press, 1954).

IDEAS COME WHEN WE LEAST EXPECT THEM

Surveys have been made as to how inventors, authors, artists, and composers receive their ideas. All seem to agree that ideas come when least expected, when people have ceased to strive for them and are half asleep or daydreaming. Some say that the idea comes *"in a flash," "out of the blue,"* while driving the car, fishing or hunting, or doing something relaxing and quite apart from work.

Many an artist has seen an entire picture in his mind and hastened to put it on canvas. The composer hears the symphony from out of nowhere with the inner ear. Mozart said of his inspiration, "Nor do I hear in my imagination the parts in sequence, but I hear them, as it were, all at once. . . . What a delight that is I cannot tell."

I, myself, arrange my best talks while watching a golf match or a football game on television. My family thinks I've lost my mind. "Why don't you get busy on your talk?" my wife asks me as I seem to waste the afternoon. Because of my legal background, I am never without a yellow lined pad. I sit down and look at the game, my yellow pad beside me, and soon—an idea comes, and then another and another. Now, the idea doesn't come from the football game, the idea comes from my subconscious mind because I have gotten my conscious mind out of the way.

A friend of mine, formerly a professor at UCLA, used to get his best ideas while pruning his roses. He was famous for the articles he wrote on medical research. After they were published, he could tell you just which roses he was working with when the ideas came through.

Paul Brunton in *The Wisdom of the Overself* locates intuition *in the deeper layer of mind beneath the threshhold of conscious thinking.*

How often have those who belong to the scribbling brotherhood woken up one morning with strange thoughts running

exultantly through their head and gotten out of bed to reproduce their ideas hastily on paper? When we remember that
numerous lines of a whole poem, Kubla Khan, worked themselves out in the sleeping mind of the poet Coleridge; that problems which agitated many a man before falling asleep were
solved immediately and spontaneously on waking again the
following morning, although they had been dismissed as insol-
uble; and that names which were forgotten and not findable
were recovered after sleep, the only and obvious conclusion is
that in some mysterious manner the mind carries on a subter-
ranean activity during the night which enables it to present a
finished result to consciousness on the following day. It is this
deeper layer of mind beneath the threshhold of conscious thinking which is the secret source of all those glorious artistic in-
spirations, all those recaptured missing links of knowledge and
all those intuitive decisions which triumph over perplexing
situations. "God giveth truth to his beloved in sleep," sung the
Biblical Psalmist. To say, therefore, in the face of proven mental activity during the sleep state that it is a lapse into total
unconsciousness, is to take only the surface value of experience
and to ignore all that lies beneath it.[4]

HOW YOU CAN INCREASE YOUR OWN CREATIVITY

My object is not to prove the existence of the Creative
Mind of the Universe. This has been done before and better.
The point to be made here is that each one of us has access
to the Creative Mind; each one is *an inlet and an outlet of
the same,* as Emerson said. The important thing for us to
learn is how to invoke the Muse. The ancient Greeks believed
that nine goddesses presided over the arts and sciences whose
favor must be won before ideas would come. Today, to muse
is a verb meaning to meditate, to contemplate, or to think
deeply. To think deeply, while at the same time being absent-
minded, would seem to be paradoxical, but that is exactly

4 Paul Brunton, *The Wisdom of the Overself,* (Philadelphia: The Blakiston
Co., 1943. Distributed by E. P. Dutton Co., Inc., New York).

how we cultivate the Creative Mind of the Universe. When we become absent from the surface mind, we are able to think deeply drawing from the vast resources of the subconscious. My dictionary, in defining the verb, to muse, describes it as *become drowned in imaginative, not too serious, reflection.*

Through Self-Direction we direct the deep subconscious mind along a certain line and if we can still the conscious mind enough to be receptive, it will go to work for us.

FOUR GOOD RULES TO FOLLOW FOR INCREASED CREATIVITY

1. *Pinpoint your thinking:*

A composer thinks about music, specifically, the kind of music in which he is interested. His mind is not focused upon physics or electronics. The artist, the scientist, the designer, the writer, all direct their attention to the particular area in which they are seeking creative ideas. If you will take one idea and live with it, you will be amazed what it will draw unto itself. Once you have opened the door, ideas will come from everywhere to clothe your original idea. Be specific as to the tack you are taking and then invite in one idea at a time.

2. *Mulling is not stewing:*

Remember, for best results you must thoroughly release your project to the subconscious mind. You are to take a lazy, lying-in-the-sun attitude as if you had all the time in the world. Toy with the ideas that come, love them, don't condemn them. Alex F. Osborn, whose book *Applied Imagination* has become the textbook used in many creative thinking courses today, maintains that it is most important not to judge the ideas as they come. "Postpone criticism," he says. He encourages groups to get together and pool their ideas, a process known as brainstorming. The cardinal rule here is never to criticize or make fun of another's idea. The same thing applies to individual brainstorming. It is a proven fact that condemnation cuts off the flow. To reject any of the ideas now will stifle the Source. There may be a time later to be selective in evaluating the ideas that have come to you.

Take it easy, busy your hands with some not too challenging occupation, watch television or listen to beautiful music if you like. All the time your deep mind will be mulling over the order given to it and soon the ideas will flow so fast you will wonder how you will ever be able to capture them all.

3. *Be prepared to seize the ideas when they come:*

Intuitive thoughts are ephemeral—fleeting, transient thoughts. They are totally unlike your habitual, limited reasoning which has become almost a part of you. These thoughts light with the delicacy of a butterfly and speed away just as quickly. They are not yet recorded on your memory track. Do not think that you will surely remember the inspiration that comes to you when you are driving the car or half asleep at night. Many a good idea has been lost in that way. Stop the car, or get up and turn on the light, whatever the case may be, and *write the idea down.*

A creative person—one who has learned to listen with the inner ear—makes a point of always having pad and pencil handy. Keep them by the bedside as ideas frequently come upon awaking or during the night. Many people train themselves to ask before retiring some question they would like to have solved, and confidently expect to be awakened by the answer they desire.

If you are a speaker or a writer, try setting up for yourself a brief outline. Go over it a few times to establish it in your mind. Now be prepared to catch the ideas that come flowing in for the next several days, or as long as you are prepared to accept them. Hang them on the "tree" you have set up and before long it will be laden down with good illustrations, far better than your usual conscious thinking could devise. Moreover, it is an easy way to work, a way that eliminates nervous tension.

4. *Now you are ready to evaluate your ideas and use them:*

Once you are through with your brainstorming session, you may be selective. This is the time to decide which of the many ideas you wish to use and eliminate the rest or store them for future reference. My own experience is that one hour of creative thinking can produce ideas useful over a long period of time. And each idea breeds more ideas, and more and more and more. Truly, intuition is our contact with the Infinite.

The late Glenn Clark wrote a book entitled *The Man Who Tapped the Secrets of the Universe.*[5] This is the story of Walter Russell, a man who said, himself, that he had five lives within his one. He excelled as a musician, an architect, an artist and sculptor, and was an illustrator of books and magazines. In 1897 and 1898 he was art editor of *Collier's Weekly* and then became war artist and correspondent for *Collier's* and *Century* during the Spanish War. In 1900, Glenn Clark reported, this remarkable man completed his allegorical painting entitled, "The Might of Ages," which was first exhibited in the Turin International Art Exposition, winning honorable mention from Italy, then exhibited throughout Europe, winning him many honors from France, Belgium, and Spain, including membership to the Spanish Academy of Arts and Letters, Toledo. He then became a great portrait painter, painting notables throughout the country. During this period he wrote a number of books and delivered hundreds of lectures. Although he never studied architecture —indeed, his formal education stopped at the age of ten—he designed and built $20 million worth of buildings in the City of New York, buildings known the world over. He financed buildings and sold all of the stock and even devised the legal possibility of cooperative ownership—which was then considered unsound.

[5] Glenn Clark, *The Man Who Tapped the Secrets of the Universe* (St. Paul, Minn.: Macalester Park Publishing Co., 1946).

At fifty-six years of age, wrote Dr. Clark, "His change from painting to sculpture came about purely because of an accident. He had been a painter all his life, and never had handled clay. He had become elected president of the Society of Arts and Sciences, and they were to give a medal to Edison. The artist who was to have done the portrait sculpturing for the medal failed them. So, Walter Russell got some clay and wired to Mrs. Edison that he would go and do it himself."

Although he later made great discoveries in science and gained an international reputation as a philosopher and lecturer, his greatest fame came through his sculptoring. Although he created many portrait busts of the great men of our times, he is best known for a group of four figures representing Freedom of Speech, Freedom of Religion, Freedom from Want, and Freedom from Fear.

"He never asked God to give him the power to do anything, for he already knew that he had that power. What he asked for in his wordless, inspirational communion was to keep forever aware of that Universal Omnipotence within him."

Do you wonder that Dr. Clark gave his book the title: *The Man Who Tapped the Secrets of the Universe?*

Walter Russell and others have tapped the secrets of the universe, but so can we. *That which Plato has known, you can know.* Intuition is not reserved for psychics, mediums, and seers. Sigmund Freud and Carl Jung considered it respectable—a normal function of the mind—but they did not discover it. The reaches of the mind have hardly been uncovered. Each one becomes a discoverer in this field. Once you have learned to listen for the voice of intuition, you will find that you can stop worrying, stop running from person to person for your answers. The Knower within you knows the solution to any problem that could ever be put before you, and unlike the answers that come through human thinking, these answers will be right answers. Try it. You may be surprised.

SELF-DIRECTION

I, too, can tap the secrets of the universe. I commune with an Infinite Source. I now open my mind to receive answers regarding [state here the particular need of the moment]. *Listening in the Silence, I am open, receptive. Inspiration wells up within me. I receive exactly the ideas that I need and with them, the Power to carry them forth into manifestation.*

VII THE POWER IN CREATIVE IMAGINATION

I rest not from my great task
To open the Eternal Worlds, to open the immortal Eyes
Of Man inwards into the Worlds of Thought: into Eternity
Ever expanding in the Bosom of God, the Human
Imagination.

WILLIAM BLAKE

WILLIAM BLAKE called the human imagination *the Bosom of God*. At first glance, this sounds a bit blasphemous; but let's see if it really is. Creative imagination is one of the most dramatic tools that God has given us. It is the means by which God creates through man and can therefore be said to be the Divine nature in man.

We have seen in Chapter VI that the Teacher within each one of us knows our needs and supplies them, a Source of unlimited ideas. It constantly provides the Guidance and Inspiration that we need when we are willing to listen. Creative imagination forms the mold through which the Creative Process of Life works to produce the manifest Universe. The chair upon which you sit was first an idea in someone's mind. This idea was translated into a visual image in that person's mind. Out of that image came the physical expression of the idea. The great Albert Einstein said, "Imagination is more important than knowledge." Ralph Waldo Emerson, the sage of Concord, wrote, "Science does not know its debt to imagination."

The science fiction books and magazines of yesteryear which seemed, at the time, to be utterly fantastic, the products of uninhibited imagination, upon review today, are often found to be fact, not fancy.

WHAT CREATIVE IMAGINATION CAN MEAN TO YOU

One can remake his entire life through the understanding and application of creative imagination. Through creative imagination it is possible to change one's belief about himself and the world in which he lives, thus changing the outpicturing of that belief. It is through creative imagination that man has progressed from level to level of accomplishment and achievement. All forward motion in our civilization has stemmed from the use of creative imagination. Spiritual growth and greater understanding come through man's use of creative imagination.

> *Where there is no vision, the people perish.*
> Proverbs 29:18

HOW THE BIBLE USES CREATIVE IMAGINATION

The Bible gives us a delightful story of how Jacob used creative imagination. Laban, Jacob's father-in-law, was not to be trusted. He had tricked Jacob before. This time Jacob was able to meet the challenge through creative imagination. Laban had agreed to give Jacob, in exchange for many years of faithful service, all of the spotted and speckled animals in his flock. But, when it came time for the fulfilling of the agreement, Laban went through the flocks first and took out all of the spotted and speckled animals and hid them, leaving none for Jacob. Jacob was not disturbed. Creative imagination won for Jacob. Where the animals went to water and to breed he set up reeds in speckled and spotted designs. And, lo, their offspring were born speckled and spotted. That which the animals beheld was reproduced in their offspring.

This is a law of life. *That to which we give our attention will be reproduced in our experience.* It behooves us to know this law and use it effectively.

MAN IS COCREATOR WITH GOD

Another way of saying this is that God creates through man.

In the beginning, God created the heaven and the earth.

And then we are told he created man, his image and likeness. Everything is already in existence, man's creation is through adapting and modifying. Through what power? Through Divine Power, of course, the only Power there is. It is all according to the thought mold man provides.

One of man's greatest blessings is that he is able to rearrange the world of effects in order to conform to his needs. Man is cocreator with God, the instrument of God, as he continually changes himself and his life through the ideas that he entertains in his mind, ideas stemming from the Source of all Life within him. God teaches man through intuition; God creates through man by means of imagination. There must always be an idea preceding the unfolding of Life. The idea opens the way.

IMAGINATION GOES BEFORE US

In my Father's house are many mansions: if it were not so, I would have told you. I go to prepare a place for you.

John 14:2

In the Universal Mind there are many states of consciousness. Each person has his own belief about himself, his ideas, and the life about him. *In my Father's house are many man-*

sions (rooms). Jesus was so sure of this that he assumed that those around him knew it too. *I go to prepare a place for you.* The Wisdom within us, creative imagination, goes ahead of us to prepare our way.

Jesus taught us, *What things soever ye desire when ye pray, believe that ye receive them, and ye shall have them.* Is this not using creative imagination? He said, *What things soever.* There were no qualifications, no conditions. Whatever it is that you desire, when you turn to the inner Source, believe that you receive it, accept it in consciousness, imagine that it is received, and you shall have it. It will surely come into your experience.

AS WITHIN, SO WITHOUT

Each one is on the pathway. Each one is endeavoring to live in accordance with the highest that is within him. Even those who seem to do things against the public good, against their own good, do so because, at that moment, they feel it is the best possible thing for them to do. But, as we lift the image of ourselves into a new dimension, we find that life about us begins to change. *And I, if I be lifted up from the earth, will draw all men unto me.*[1] As we lift our consciousness to a higher dimension, we find that life about us conforms to the new concept. This is creative imagination at work!

HOW DO WE USE CREATIVE IMAGINATION?

There are many ways. I am going to give you two ways. Usually, we are told to start right where we are with what we have, but this time I am going to suggest you start from the end and not the beginning. That sounds strange, doesn't it?

[1] John 12:32.

It is a little different twist, but actually we are saying the same thing. You really do start right where you are with what you have. It is all in what you have. Do you have an image of failure, or incompleteness, or do you have an image of fulfillment? When we start with our highest good, knowing that that which we are seeking is established in consciousness through the law of creative imagination, all of the steps in between will be taken care of to bring about complete fulfillment.

Another way to say this is that when we pray we do not allow ourselves to become involved in the lack. We do not become involved in the disease, or the trouble. When we pray we turn to the Highest, knowing that all of the things in between will be provided. Emmet Fox called this using the Golden Key. Turn away from the difficulty and turn the attention to God, he said. This is the *summum bonum,* the highest good, the alpha and omega, the beginning and the end. This is *seek ye first the kingdom of God* (within) *and all of these things shall be added.*

HOW A PRINCE USED CREATIVE IMAGINATION

There is an old legend about a prince who had a crooked back. Because the prince was very sensitive about his deformity he seldom appeared among his people. One day he called the royal sculptor and told him that he wanted him to make a beautiful statue of him as he would be without his deformity. The sculptor went to work. In due time the prince was presented with a beautiful image in marble exactly as he would like to look. The prince was delighted. He put the statue in a secret nook in the garden and every day he went there and contemplated himself as he would really like to be. Month after month, he went there alone and each time when he returned he was able to stand a little bit more erect. Several years passed. Finally, he called a meeting of all his subjects. From far and wide they came to see their prince. This time he gladly appeared before them. Lo and behold! when the people looked at him they could hardly believe their eyes. The prince no longer had a crooked back. He had kept always before him the vision of a perfect back and this ideal image had become manifest in his experience.

EVERY GREAT INVENTOR USES CREATIVE IMAGINATION

Eli Whitney was a graduate of Yale University, a young man who liked to tinker. After his graduation from Yale he was invited down to Savannah, Georgia to visit in the home of Nathaniel Greene, one of the Generals in the Revolutionary War. While there, someone pointed out to him the great problem involved in picking the seeds out of cotton. Have you ever tried to pick the seeds out of cotton? They are embedded in the middle of the white fiber and it takes many minutes to disengage just one seed. Cotton, at that time, was costly to produce because man lacked a way to disengage the seeds. But this young man, just out of college, thought, "This is a problem that has an answer." Immediately he set to, to find the answer, visualizing the seed separated from the cotton. In other words, he put the idea into Mind, and soon he began to see that it could be accomplished very simply. Within a few days he had worked out a gadget that was able to clean, in one day, fifty pounds of cotton—an accomplishment that was to the people of that day a miracle. Eli Whitney was at that time only twenty-four years of age. Thrilled with his victory, he went back up North and set up a factory to make the cotton gin. For years his company was behind in its orders, so great was the demand. Where there is an idea there is always fulfillment if creative imagination is used with persistence.

We do not all choose to be inventors. However, creative

imagination can be used in many ways, in the simple things of life.

PRAYER IS THE HIGHEST FORM OF CREATIVE IMAGINATION

God works through prayer, using our creative imagination for the purpose of disengaging our minds from old concepts that have been entangling us, that we may open them to receive the creative impress from the Source of all Wisdom, allowing the new idea to take form in our life.

An example of this is using scientific power for another. Suppose an individual comes to us who seems to have the burdens of the world upon his shoulders. He feels that everything is against him. We must disengage the old picture, see the person whole and free. Through creative imagination we now behold a spiritual being filled with Power. Once we have seen behind the mortal façade, beholding him a divine, perfect, spiritual being, the image and likeness of his Maker, nothing can keep this Truth from prevailing.

YOU ARE WHAT YOU THINK

In the same way, we must see ourselves as stepping out into a new life, the kind of life we would like to live. If we have thought of ourselves as being unhealthy, habitually tired, discouraged, and unhappy, we must change that picture. Thoughts are things. The pattern of our thinking today is making our tomorrows. Once we understand this, we will think twice before indulging in a bout of self-pity. We will actually stand in awe of the Law of Life to such an extent that we would rather take a dose of poison than wallow in old patterns of negative thinking.

There is a popular saying, *you are what you eat*. Far more important, *you are what you think*. That which you believe about yourself is sure to become your experience. *That which you contemplate you become.* Let your imagination be a means of looking up and not down, looking toward the Infinite, opening the mind to receive the creative impress of Universal Life. Through the power of creative imagination, there is no goal too great to be achieved, no dream impossible. "If one advances confidently in the direction of his dreams and endeavors to live the life he has imagined, he will meet success unexpected in common hours," wrote Henry Thoreau.

Do not be afraid to dream. Dreams are the stuff from which life is made; but, having dreamed, believe in your dreams, visualize them as having already taken place in the world of sight and sound and touch. Imagine yourself as having already achieved perfect health. Hear yourself telling your friends and relatives, "I feel wonderful!" Imagine yourself saying over and over, "This has been a wonderful year. I have been successful in everything I have undertaken!"

Einstein said that imagination is more important than knowledge. William Blake called it God. I say that imagination is God in action.

SELF-DIRECTION

I feel wonderful! I am a strong, healthy person. I enjoy good health.
Only good goes from me and only good returns to me.
I attract wonderful friends into my experience.
The clients I need, the clients who need me, are directed to my door.
I use my imagination constructively, visualizing that which I wish to experience.
All my dreams are realized in wonderful ways!

VIII HOW TO BUILD CONFIDENCE IN YOURSELF

Confidence is that feeling by which the mind embarks in great and honorable courses with a sure hope and trust in itself.

CICERO, *Rhetorical Invention*

WE all realize the need for building self-confidence. There are Toastmaster's Clubs, Gavelmaster's Clubs, salesmanship classes, and human relations classes. All these and more are devoted to this need of the individual to develop a sense of confidence in himself.

But, when people say that they lack self-confidence, are they all talking about the same thing? Some people lack confidence in themselves when they are required to speak before an audience. There are some who lack confidence in their ability to drive an automobile. The late Don Blanding was perfectly at home on the speaker's platform, but he did not have confidence in his ability to drive an automobile. The great Ty Cobb was poised, confident, and at home on a baseball diamond, but afraid to make a speech of any kind. Which simply shows that a person can have self-confidence in one field and not in another. There are those who lack confidence in sports. Some lack confidence in getting along with other people. Somewhere along the line, most people lack confidence in some area in their lives.

OVERCOMING SELF-CONSCIOUSNESS

Whenever the attention is centered upon an individual, that person is apt to become uneasy or self-conscious. The focus of attention upon a person tends to unnerve him. When one is conscious of the self, he tends to lose his self-confidence. The mere fact that someone is looking on, perhaps critically, often causes one to lose his poise and to become aware of his limitations. Fear creeps in. Fear is a process that one sets up to protect himself. An example of this is the talented artist or musician who avoids pursuing his art lest he should be a failure in the eyes of others. Fear causes one to do and say things that he'd rather not express, and to be uncomfortable and awkward when he would rather be relaxed and poised. Everybody wants to get rid of this crippling fear so that he can walk into any situation with his head held high, with a feeling of confidence and assurance.

WHISTLING IN THE DARK

There is a lot of difference between confidence and cockiness. Confidence is a feeling of assurance about life, it is an inward knowing that one can rely on himself in any circumstance. When a person is conceited or cocky he is trying to convince others that he has self-confidence which he doesn't really have. He is really insecure and is whistling in the dark. Such a person has a greater insecurity than the person who is just self-conscious.

FEAR OF FAILURE

One of the fears causing one to lose confidence in himself is the fear of failure. Each person wants to succeed. Take the athlete who wants to succeed so much that he develops a fear that something will happen to cause him to fail during the course of the event. This fear of failure can react upon the athlete in one of two ways; to spur him on to greater achievement in order that he won't fail, or if he gives in to the fear of failure he may find himself losing confidence. Then his ability begins to slip away.

I am reminded of a golf match I followed several years ago. It was the final day of a big tournament. A large amount of money and prestige hinged on every stroke. A certain player was leading the pack. Because he was leading, he became more conscious of the consequences of a possible mistake. One could see that he was becoming more and more tense as the play progressed. Still, it appeared he was going to win the tournament, for he was playing a methodical game. At the sixteenth hole the excitement was really running high. He got onto the green and the other members of the threesome were also on the green. Our potential champion had a long putt to make. I watched him line up the putt, the very picture of concentration. He had everything under control, the line of the putt, the speed of the green, the contour of the green. In other words, he had "read the green," and was ready to make his putt. As he drew back his putter to stroke the ball a movie camera started right at his elbow. "B-r-r-r, b-r-r-r, b-r-r-r." The man immediately drooped. I have never seen a person so deflated, so bewildered. He had given no thought to the gallery watching his every movement until this movie camera called his attention to it. At that moment he couldn't go through with the putt. He just stood there.

Finally, he was able to hit the ball; but, he was a different player. He had become self-conscious. He finished the tournament, but he lost it. Why? Because he became conscious of himself and thereby lost his self-confidence. The fear of failure came in. He began to think of what would happen if he didn't make the putt. Well, he didn't have long to wonder. He missed that putt and several others. Like Job, *what he greatly feared came to pass.*

FEAR OF RIDICULE

Then, we have another fear, the fear of appearing ridiculous. This causes many people to lose confidence. We all want to appear poised. We want to appear self-assured, certainly not ridiculous. There's the girl who is afraid that her slip will show and when she finds at the end of the day that it has, she blushes to think of it. There's the man who went to a party in a sport shirt and found everyone else in tuxedos. Years later whenever he thought of it, his self-confidence was shaken as he thought, "How ridiculous I must have looked!" So many times little things happen in our lives that make us appear ridiculous. All of a sudden the attention is on us; we get self-conscious and we blush and stammer.

"THAT MAN KICKED ME!"

Here is another fear, the fear of exposing the ego to hurts. The ego is very sensitive and always looking for hurts. A friend of ours, recounts this story: He told of having gone into one of those narrow diner lunch stands. He said that in going down the narrow aisle, somehow or other he managed to brush against a woman who had her foot a little way out in the aisle. He turned back to apologize and heard her say in a complaining sort of a voice, "That man kicked me!"

He begged her pardon and went on to his seat. As he walked away he heard her muttering over and over, "Somebody's *always* kicking me!" She had a consciousness of *somebody's always kicking me* and so someone always obliged her. I imagine all of you who read this know some person who is always being kicked by someone. Such a person needs to regain his self-confidence.

The ego is the little outer self, the personality self, which we have developed over the years. The word personality comes from the Latin word *persona* meaning "mask." It is the mask or façade that we present to the world, hoping that the world will think it real. We don't want anyone to look behind that mask or façade lest they see a quivering, insecure, little person there. Therefore, we often live in terror that the ego or personality mask will be hurt or exposed, and will go to almost any length to protect it.

FEAR OF BEING REJECTED

Another fear is the fear of being rejected. A classic example is the shy young man about to ask a young lady for a date. We picture him red in the face, stammering, thoroughly embarrassed and self-conscious. He is unable to speak fluently. He is miserable. We joke about it but it is no joke to him. His is the fear of being rejected, the fear of being pushed away. There is a complete lack of self-confidence involved in this situation. The fear of being rejected runs through many parts of life. Some people are afraid to make friends and lead lonely lives in order to protect themselves from the possibility of being rejected.

Psychologists have found that this fear of being rejected is one of the key problems in marital relationships. Because of this fear, often one party in the marital relationship will not give the whole self into the marriage. There is a holding back. A good marriage must be based on hundred-percent giving from each marriage partner, and not the attitude of: "I want your love and devotion, as much as I can get; but I won't give you mine for fear I will get hurt." We hear a lot about fifty-fifty giving in marriage. This sort of giving is still a contest based on self-protection.

FEAR OF DISAPPROVAL

Then, there is the fear of loss of approval. The child learns a little rhyme and goes before the parents to recite. The parents are not pleased as the child had expected them to be. Perhaps they may criticize the method of delivery. The child immediately feels the disapproval of the parents—becomes self-conscious and loses confidence in himself. The memory of this experience often reflects into his future life.

Many times parents set higher standards than the child is able to achieve, thereby causing the child to strain at life. The problem of stammering often results from the perfection demanded by parents. Stammering is often caused by self-consciousness based on the fear of loss of approval.

The fear of loss of approval is not a problem of children only. We find it running through every phase of human experience. Many people will refrain from expressing their real talents because of the fear of the lack of approval of their fellow men. This fear explains the tendency of man to shrink from originality of thought and conform blindly to the average thinking of the majority. In our civilization today, we have made almost a fetish of the desirability of being "normal." Finally, a man loses confidence in his ability to think for himself. The newspaper becomes his Bible, and the approval of his fellows his highest goal in life. He thereby loses his true identity.

We find this to be a basic problem with the alcoholic. He drinks to be a good fellow and to be approved by his friends. Therefore, he accepts drinks that at first he does not really desire. Later, they become a necessity to bolster his ego. The fear of loss of approval causes a lack of confidence in the self. The alcohol gives him a false self-confidence.

FEAR OF ADVERSE CONSEQUENCES

What about the fear of adverse consequences? I have known people who would not dare start out on a new venture for fear that the consequences of that venture might be adverse, and this they could not face.

I knew a man in San Francisco, the manager of a very large business, who was not only an excellent manager, but well liked by everyone. When faced with getting new business for his company, he would become panicky. The sad thing was that this company was already so prosperous there was no need for this panic. It really didn't matter whether they got additional business or not. And yet, the moment he turned his attention to getting new business, he would become a different person, apprehensive, lacking confidence in himself. He would go from one person to another asking, "How do you think this should be done?" They would conscientiously try to give him advice, little knowing that he had already gone to ten or twelve others to ask them the same thing, and that when he left he would go to someone else, imparting the same feeling of uncertainty. One time, in the midst of just such a project, he took his own life. The fear of adverse consequences became too much for him.

WHERE ARE WE PLACING OUR TRUST?

Now, we have discussed lack of self-confidence pretty thoroughly. We have found that a lack of self-confidence is a feeling that everything depends on the limited, human self. Now, what is the opposite? This depends on the answer to a question—are you self-conscious or Self-conscious? Where are we placing our trust? I could not tell anyone how to find confidence in the personality or little self, *man whose breath is in his nostrils.* The Bible says, *With men this is impossible; but with God all things are possible.*[1] True self-confidence is Self-confidence, or confidence in the Perfect Power within.

Now what is this Self in which we are to have perfect trust? It is Infinite Intelligence that knows all the answers and can meet every problem that may arise in our lives. It is Love that will not leave us unprotected; that comes to our rescue

[1] Matthew 19:26.

every time and will never let us be hurt. It is Almighty Power stepped down into our lives as the strength to do all that we need to do.

The first step in building Self-confidence is to get the human self out of the way. Jesus understood this when he said, *I can of mine own self do nothing.* Here was a man who truly had Self-confidence. He dared to cast out demons, heal all manner of disease, feed the multitude, and even raise the dead. And yet, he admitted *of himself he could do nothing.* True Self-confidence starts with this admission. With Jesus it was knowing that a Power greater than he, working within him, did the works. Jesus had Self-confidence because he believed that nothing was impossible to the Power within. To men it was impossible. He told us: *Verily, verily, I say unto you, He that believeth on me, the works that I do shall he do also; and greater works than these shall he do; because I go unto my Father.* Here is the clue that most people pass right by. We are not to struggle with our human strength and intelligence; but, to *go unto the Father* who is the Source of all Power and Intelligence. Perhaps it will be helpful to paraphrase the words of Jesus, "Of my human self I can do nothing, the Intelligence within me doeth the works."

THERE IS A WAY TO BUILD CONFIDENCE

How do you build confidence in yourself? The first and foremost thing that we have to know is that everything comes from within. *All Power belongeth unto God—Thine is the Power and Thine is the glory.* We are not separate from this Power. As Jesus said, *All Power is given unto me in heaven* (within) *and in earth* (outer manifestation). Everything in heaven (the invisible side of Life,) and in earth (the outer manifestation) that we know so well, comes from the One Source, which Jesus called *the Father.* The very food that we eat is Substance Spirit stepped down into visible manifestation. The very air we breathe is Spirit surrounding us and sustaining us. *In Spirit we live and move and have our being.*

SELF-CONFIDENCE APPLIED IN MANY FIELDS

Let us take public speaking, an art that requires considerable Self-confidence. Jesus told his disciples, when they were going out into the field to preach the gospel and to heal the sick, that if they were ever brought before the tribunal that they should not premeditate what they should say, but that they should trust the Spirit, and at that very hour the Spirit would tell them what to say. *When they deliver you up, take no thought how or what ye shall speak: for it shall be given you in that same hour what ye shall speak. For it is not ye that speak, but the Spirit of your Father which speaketh in you.* With this thought, all self-consciousness vanishes and true Self-confidence takes hold. It is right and proper that one should study and practice in order to learn good techniques. It is well to prepare through research the material upon which one desires to speak. These are necessary human footsteps; but, take no anxious thought, the Inspiration and the Power and the Intelligence come from within.

In everything that we do, whether it be in business, in the home, in the schoolroom, or wherever we are, we should realize that we are expressing Life and that this Life is Infinite and Perfect. This Life that we are expressing is one with all Life; therefore, there is no separation between God and man, or man and man. We are all One in Mind.

The piano player who lets the music flow through his fingers, the writer who holds the pen so that the Creative Mind can be expressed through him are both expressing Beauty at their point of use. "All writing comes by the grace of God, and all doing and having," wrote Emerson. Yes, it is well to practice and study, to prepare for whatever career one undertakes; but, when one studies, he is using Universal Mind.

Without Infinite Intelligence which is expressed through him, the studying would be impossible. True greatness and all Inspiration come from getting the little self out of the way and letting the Divine Self shine through.

CASTING OUT FEAR

God is Love, the self-givingness of the Spirit, everywhere present, being expressed through Its creation. This perfect Love casts out fear. Without this recognition of Love, right where we are, we feel separated from Life, alone and struggling, faced with a cruel and competitive world. Self-confidence is reliance upon the Self within, the divine Spirit of God right where we are. As we have faith in the Power and Intelligence within us, we can do all things. *With men it is impossible; but to God all things are possible.*[2]

Paul was able to face all forms of trial and tribulation to the glory of God because he realized this Truth, *I can do all things through Christ which strengtheneth me,*[3] he said. He had Self-confidence because he knew that nothing depended on Paul, the man. *I live; yet not I, Christ* (the individualized Spirit within) *liveth in me.*[4]

The man, Jesus, never healed anyone; but to Jesus the Christ all things were possible. In each instance he turned to the Father, that Perfect Power within him and received the Power he needed. *The son doeth what he seeth the Father do,*[5] he said. *The works that I do shall he do also; and greater works than these shall he do.*[6]

2 Matthew 19:26.
3 Philippians 4:13.
4 Galatians 2:20.
5 John 5:19.
6 John 14:12.

WHO CAN BE AGAINST US?

Behold what manner of love the Father hath bestowed upon us, that we should be called the sons of God.[7] The true Self within each one of us is the Christ Self, the son of God, to whom all things are possible. We do not have to struggle hopelessly, battling a heartless and unsympathetic world. We do not have to depend upon man *whose breath is in his nostrils.*[8] We are never alone. The Infinite is always with us. The whole world may seem to be against us; but *if God be for us, who can be against us.*[9] At any moment we can turn within to the Power that knows no defeat and be lifted up where we will draw all men unto us. The Perfect Power within knows no limitation. Infinite Intelligence has all the answers and can, through each one of us, preach a sermon, give a talk, or write a book that would amaze us. Self-consciousness comes from depending on the human self and wondering what other humans will think of our endeavors. Self-confidence comes from depending on the Power that is able to do all things for us, accomplishing feats beyond our imagination with Inspiration and Enthusiasm.

POWER THROUGH MEDITATION

Start your day with at least fifteen minutes of meditating upon the wonder and the glory of God in your life. Turn away from the challenges of the day and read the Bible or some other inspirational literature. Take with you all through the day the inspiring thoughts that come to you at this time. Let this meditation period be your point of contact with your Source as though you had had your daily conference with

7 John 3:1.
8 Isaiah 2:22.
9 Romans 8:31.

your Superior. Now step forth into your life experience and live the kind of Life you have been wanting to live with complete Self-confidence. The Spirit of Truth within you will teach you all that you need to know and lead you into paths of perfect right action. It is well to return to one's Source as many times as possible throughout the day. It is the pause that truly refreshes. Come back for instructions. A moment or two will do. Say to the Father within, "All right, Father, what shall I do next?" or "Speak, Lord, thy servant heareth." Listen for a moment and, when you have received your Inspiration, live on with confidence and enthusiasm. *In returning and rest shall ye be saved, in quietness and confidence shall be your strength.*[10]

We must be willing to follow the instructions that come from within. Perhaps we will be led to give a different talk from the one which we had prepared. Perhaps the house we build will not be what we thought we wanted at all, or the dress we purchase not the one we set out to buy. But, the end result is always so much better when we trust our inner Guidance, which will never fail us or forsake us.

I cannot stress too much the importance of loving the Life within and trusting it completely. Sometimes this seems a difficult thing for people who have gotten into the habit of fearing circumstances and their fellows. We must be willing to forsake false motives, such as striving for success in order to get ahead of others, or to prove ourselves right. In order to build true Self-confidence, we must be willing to give all the glory to the Power within. By so doing, we give up our fears for they cannot exist in the Presence of God. Self-confidence is always accompanied by enthusiasm which gives sparkle to life. Enthusiasm is derived from the Greek words *en theos,* meaning "in God." As we live enthusiastically, we are one with Him and nothing can defeat us. *If ye abide in me and*

10 Isaiah 30:15.

*my words abide in you, ye shall ask what ye will, and it shall
be done unto you.*[11]

*Trust in the Lord with all thine heart; and lean not unto
thine own understanding. In all thy ways acknowledge Him
and He shall direct thy paths.*[12] By completely relying upon
Omnipotent Power, Infinite Love and Intelligence, we can
move into any experience with a sense of inner assurance and
perfect peace. *The battle is not ours but the Lord's.*[13] This is
truly the way to build Self-confidence. It is total reliance on
the Perfect Power within which does all things through us,
for us. We no longer need to protect the troublesome ego
when we trust; therefore, we have nothing to lose and everything to gain. Once we find this inner Security, we can never
lack confidence again. Once we have true Self-confidence we
have opened the door for Infinite Intelligence to be expressed
freely through us without being stifled by the crippling fear
of human self-consciousness.

Yes, *it is better to trust in the Lord than to put confidence
in man,*[14] and hereon lies the whole answer. What are we
really seeking? If it is important to us to appease the human
ego with praise and adulation, then we are doomed to failure,
fear, and disappointment. It is only when we get what Emerson called "our bloated nothingness" out of the way of the
divine circuit that we are able to achieve true Self-confidence.

**PERHAPS WE SHOULD ASK OURSELVES—
"WHAT ARE WE REALLY SEEKING?"**

The one thing we need is not that other people will like us
better; but that we shall love them more.
This is true Self-confidence.
Not that we should strive to make peace between countries so

11 John 15:7.
12 Proverbs 3:5, 6.
13 II Chronicles 20:15.
14 Psalms 118:8.

that we shall not have to fear war; but that we shall find peace within our own confused selves.

This is true Self-confidence.

Not that we should work to gain the applause of a fickle world; but that we should be satisfied with the effort we ourselves are making to please God within.

This is true Self-confidence.

Not that we should set the world on fire with our recognized successes; but that we should find the real wealth of the Spirit within that can never know failure.

This is true Self-confidence.

KEY THOUGHT FOR BUILDING SELF-CONFIDENCE

To men it is impossible, but to God all things are possible. The Perfect Power within me, can do all things with ease and with certainty. I let the Perfect Power speak through me and act for me.

SELF-DIRECTION FOR SELF-CONFIDENCE

I cease fearing failure. I now live for the sheer joy of living. I rely on and trust the Creative Power within me.

I trust God, not only within me, but within everyone. No one can reject me because I am one with all of Life.
I accept Life joyfully and lovingly.
I am accepted by Life right now.

Spirit within me sustains me at all times, giving me a feeling of serenity and assurance.
Wherever I am, whatever I am doing, the Infinite Presence is there living through me in It's Perfect Way.

IX DECISION MAKING CAN BE A CINCH!

He that will not command his thoughts will soon lose the command of his actions.

THOMAS WILSON

Wнo makes *your* decisions?

If thine eye be single, thy whole body shall be full of light said a great man. James considered the double-minded man unstable in all his ways, comparing him to a wave of the sea, driven with the wind and tossed. Both understood that it was important to make decisions and then stick with them. When we back away and start in another direction, giving one order one moment and another the next, the subconscious mind does not know how to proceed.

We have seen how Psychogenesis works. Now we are going to learn how to give directions that will enable us to be decisive.

THE VALUE OF BEING MORE DECISIVE

Suppose a family is ready to take a vacation. The father has been given vacation time by his employer. They have the money in the bank for a trip. "But where shall we go?" they say. "I'd like to go fishing," the father says. "I'd like to go to the mountains," says Mother. "Let's go to Disneyland!" shout the children. Day after day they argue and no decision is reached. Or, if they start out for the mountains, they go only a little way before Father's idea prevails and they turn back toward the lake; but before they reach the lake, the children have made such a fuss that the parents agree it would be better to turn back toward Disneyland to keep peace in the family. Meantime, they are wasting their vacation by failing to come to a decision. This is an example of how the thoughts in one's own mind go round and round in trying to make a decision. The person who is unable to make a decision never gets far in any direction.

The subconscious mind is continually executing the orders given it by the conscious mind. But what about those orders? We have found that the subconscious mind responds to the order to the extent that it is believed by the conscious mind. Where there is indecision, where the mind is pointing in one direction one moment and another direction the next moment, the subconscious mind gets completely confused. It no sooner starts out to fill one order than it receives another. It wants to comply. It knows only to be the faithful servant, but what is it going to do?

One of the ways we can train our minds is to learn to be more decisive. Man has been given the power of choice. It is up to him to use it. When we hesitate to make a choice because we fear we may not make the right choice, this indecisiveness binds the subconscious mind. It causes that wonderful, efficient order taker to reach an impasse and nothing is accomplished in any direction.

A SHORT CUT TO DECISIVENESS

The person who would develop decisiveness must make up his mind that he is going to make a decision. Say to the self: "I am now making a decision." Maybe your decision will be to procrastinate, but at least you will do it decisively! There are times when your inner guidance will tell you that it is better to wait. You will be told by that still, small voice within you "this is not the time." This, however, is different from floundering in a sea of indecisiveness. When we turn to the Wisdom within for our guidance, we will be told what to do and how to do it. Not only will we be given right choices, but right timing. The important thing is that we make up our minds to trust our guidance and act upon it. When the green light comes, we must be ready to move. "I am now making a decision" is the first step.

HOW THIS REVELATION CAME TO ME

Sometimes there are decisions to be made where several roads seem equally desirable. It is hard to know just which turn to take. Once in my life, I had come to such a place. I would not call it a dilemma exactly, because I have learned not to worry and stew about these things. But there was a crossroad, and each road led to a cul-de-sac or blind alley. I did not know which road to take. There were several possible courses and yet none of them seemed right. I should make a move and yet the answer did not seem clear to me.

This is the time when many people lie awake at night, call all of their friends for advice, get out the Ouija board, or consult a fortuneteller—all equally unproductive steps. I sat down and had a good meditation.

THE PERSONAL FACTOR

In my own case, I saw that I had only to direct the divine Intelligence within me to make the decision for me. This I did in my meditation, something like this:

"Perfect Intelligence within me, my divine and perfect Self, I am directing You to make this decision for me. I know that You are one with the Universal All-Knowing Mind, that knows all answers. Therefore, You know how to choose the way that blesses all, that brings each facet of this work into divine perfect harmonious right action. My direction is *Let Thy Perfect Will Be Done in and Through Me. Let the Right Decision Be Made in and Through Me. Let Thy Perfect Will Be Done in Its Perfect Way."*

After that, I felt a wonderful sense of release. I knew that I didn't have to do another thing until my orders came through. Then, I would be told from within what to do and how to do it each step of the way. It wasn't long before the decision came to me just as clear as a bell. I had let the Wisdom within me make it in the right way through Self-Direction. Before, I had been literally choosing indecision.

THOUGHTS THAT MAKE US STRONG

It is through the doorway of thought that the outer expression of life is determined. As Kahlil Gibran said in *The Prophet*, "Much of our pain is self-chosen." We need not be weak and fearful, poor or sick. Through Self-Direction we are privileged to start an entirely new train of action in our experience. We are not at the mercy of the physical or material existence. We have access to the Infinite; but even God cannot work for us unless He works through us. We have been given the power of choice. Each must chart his course and listen for right Guidance in order to make right decisions.

AN EXERCISE IN DECISIVENESS

A good way to stop floundering in the sea of indecision is to use a pencil and paper. If you have a decision to make, sit down with paper and pencil and start writing down the various alternatives, the various decisions you could come to, the pros and cons under each. This brings a sense of order into the thinking. Now back away a bit and without jumping from one alternative to another, ask your subconscious mind (which is your inlet and your outlet of the great Universal

Mind) to guide you in making the right decision. We all know that when we fail to remember a person's name, the harder we try to remember, the more it eludes us, but when we release it, back away from it for a moment, it quickly pops into mind, so do we approach this business of making a decision.

Having written down the various alternatives and having asked for guidance, we now turn to some other activity—read a book, look at television, take a walk—release the problem at hand. Many people ask for guidance before going to sleep at night and with their waking thought the answer comes. The answer will come. It will feel good and it will be right as of the moment. Maybe in the last analysis you will alter your course. At that time you will make a decision to alter your course. This is good. Life is continually changing and we must be flexible, but this is entirely different from the morass of indecisive thinking that gets one nowhere.

HOW TO TAKE DOMINION OF YOUR LIFE AND AFFAIRS

The subconscious mind responds to feeling. Much of the direction we give it is by feeling—how we feel about this life that we are living. Decisiveness is a matter of feeling. Refuse to let yourself feel uneasy, muddled, and insecure. Know that there are answers to every problem and that these answers are available to you. Life is a series of choices from the moment we start out in the morning until we choose to go to sleep at night. We choose how we will have our eggs in the morning, we choose what tie we will wear, we choose our attitudes each moment of the day. All that we see and experience is the result of these choices, these beliefs about ourselves. It is up to us whether we develop confidence in ourselves. It is up to us how we approach our lives. As the poet said, we are the masters of our fate and the captains of our souls. It is time we realized this and took dominion, that God-given dominion to which we are entitled. It is only through Self-Direction that we can take dominion in our lives. Decision making is a cinch once we take control.

> *One ship sails East, another West,*
> *By the self-same winds that blow;*
> *'Tis the set of the sail and not the gale,*
> *That determines the way they go.*
> Ella Wheeler Wilcox

We set the sails that will weather the gales when we choose that which we really want to experience instead of that which we would like to be rid of. Suppose a person is unemployed. He thinks that he is at a crossroad. He doesn't know which way to go. "I can't make a decision until I find a job," he says. His every thought contributes to his unemployment, his feeling of complete futility. His first step is to make the decision to be employed, to be a person with a good occupation, with right remuneration. If he continues to give his subconscious mind the order, "I will get a job at some future date," the subconscious mind won't be able to do anything for him. Tomorrow never comes. Tomorrow is always tomorrow. He should start out by claiming, "I am employed. There is a right job for me. I am making a decision to go to work and it is now revealed to me where that work is." Now, the subconscious mind has something to work on and all of Life will go to work to make this decision a reality. That which we believe about ourselves is the order that we give to the subconscious mind. As long as a person thinks of himself as unemployed, that will be his experience.

The same thing is true about health, companionship, memory, or any other facet of our livingness. The person who constantly tells himself (and others, usually) that he is sick, suffering, susceptible to every bug that comes along, will find that he is ailing most of the time; while the person who boasts that he comes from healthy stock, has never been sick a day in his life, etc., will be the picture of health and vigor. Why do some lead lonely lives while others find just the right companion? Why do some people have poor memories while others can remember whatever they wish? Life does not discriminate against us, we discriminate against ourselves by the poor orders that we give our subconscious minds. It is up to us to take dominion in a decisive way.

SELF-DIRECTION
IN MAKING A DECISION

I am a decisive person. Through the Wisdom within me I am able to make wise choices. The Intelligence within me knows what is right for me and guides me in making these choices. My subconscious mind is one with the Universal Mind and thus I am assured that all of Life is working with me. In the Universal Mind there is a perfect plan for me and it is revealed to me as I open my mind to receive it. I now accept the perfect answer as it comes to me from within. The Wisdom within me makes my decisions. I trust these decisions. I move forward calmly and confidently into paths of right action.

X PROSPERITY THRIVES
ON SELF-DIRECTION

*That which you can conceive of, believe in, and confi-
dently expect, must necessarily become your experience.*

TRUE prosperity is an awareness of the Abundance of Life.
Such an awareness would include all of the added things at
the relative level. The word *prosper* actually means *to flour-
ish; to succeed; to thrive; to experience good or favorable
results.* Each person's measure of prosperity must be particular to that individual. Therefore, to prosper does not necessarily mean to have a great fortune, although making money
can well be one of the by-products of a prosperity consciousness. However, just as soon as we begin to measure income,
we are working in the realm of the relative. True prosperity
is Absolute. It starts with an inner dominion that causes one
to prosper at every level of his experience. It includes abundance at every level. It includes right action and complete
fulfillment. What we are seeking, then, is a consciousness of
true prosperity, an inner dominion through an awareness of
the Perfect Power within us. In developing this awareness
we must consider five basic principles.

THE FIVE BASIC PRINCIPLES OF TRUE PROSPERITY

1. God's Love for us is not conditioned by person, place,
   condition, thing, or circumstance.
2. It is up to each one of us to erase the circle of self-
   imposed limitation and let the Infinite live through us.

3. Every man individualizes the Infinite through the speaking of his word.
4. The Law is: that which you can conceive of, believe in, and confidently expect must necessarily become your experience.
5. As you give, Life will give back to you; all of Life is one with you.

There is no question in my mind about the soundness of these five principles. If you will study them, live with them, practice them, and come to understand them, you will never know lack again. You will finally come to have an inner security manifested as an ever increasing abundance of good.

Remember: *That which you can conceive of, believe in, and confidently expect, must necessarily become your experience.*

This is a law of life! It does not matter who you are. The law is no respecter of persons. It does not care who you are, what your background may have been, your nationality, or race. It works entirely through consciousness. That which you can believe about yourself is sure to become your experience.

Here's a little story that illustrates what I'm talking about. For the third time the fisherman took a large trout off his hook and threw it back into the stream. With the next cast he drew in a fingerling, a small trout no longer than his index finger. With a big smile he took it off the hook and stuck it in his creel.

The man who was fishing beside him could stand it no longer, "You caught three nice trout and threw them all back," he exclaimed, "but now you keep this little one not much larger than a sardine! I don't understand it!"

"Yep, small frying pan," was the terse reply.

Sometimes, a little story like this can point up a great truth.

Man is continually selling himself short because he has a small evaluation of his own capabilities. In the Bible, the word "fish" stands for ideas. How many expansive ideas have you thrown back into the sea of mind because you couldn't make room for them in your thinking?

GOD'S LOVE FOR US IS NOT CONDITIONED

Many people habitually feel that Life is against them. This is not true. Life loves us and wants us to have the best. In one of Paul's letters he said: *Be not conformed to this world: but be ye transformed by the renewing of your mind, that ye may prove what is that good, and acceptable, and perfect, will of God.* This chapter is designed to help us renew our minds that we may accept our rightful place in life. We are going to build a greater consciousness that will enable us to take dominion over our lives. Prosperity, like breathing, is natural. We have only to uncover that which already is, be our real selves, and accept our good in mind. The will of God for us is always for our greatest good. Nothing is withheld. We alone have closed the door on our good.

OUR LIMITATION IS SELF-IMPOSED

The great Socrates told his students: "As for me, all I know is that I know nothing." Among the many ideas that I owe to Socrates is the one I am about to share with you.

Take a sheet of white paper and draw a circle on it. Did you draw a small circle, or a large circle? This is revealing, a clear indication of whether one has a limited or an expansive consciousness. Now, as near to the center of the circle as you can, place a dot. The dot represents your point of awareness in the infinite realm of Universal Mind. You are the center of your world. The circle represents the limitation that you place upon infinite Life living through you. It will be interesting to you to note how large a circle you drew in the first place. Some will draw minute circles, others will extend their circle to the limit of the page.

Now, erase the circle. It will no longer matter whether it was small or large. You now have only the dot left. You are now the center of a circle without a circumference. This, by the way, was Socrates' definition of man—*the center of a circle without a circumference.* By erasing the circle you have eliminated the boundary of your world and entered into the infinite Life of Mind.

As you contemplate the faint tracing of the circle just erased, ask yourself, "What were the limitations that I had imposed upon myself? Have I been continually saying, 'It can't be done?' Have I accepted for myself a circumscribed income? A limitation of being too old to accomplish certain things? Have I set up for myself barriers of lack of education, class limitation, limitation of race or environment?"

Now, you have erased those limitations even as you erased the circle. As you look at the dot, you see that you are the center of an infinite Life in which you can relate yourself to the wholeness of life without subtracting or detracting from any other part of life. Always remember, that dot in the center represents you. You are an infinite being, without boundaries, kept from expressing your infinite nature only because you had a circle of limitation around you. Just as you erased the circle of limitation on the paper, so can you erase the circle of limitation in your mind, for it is a circle representing the confines of your own belief, your own limited thinking about yourself. Whether it was large or small, it is your circle. You drew that circle of limitation around yourself. You, alone, kept it there through the years by your "I can'ts," and other forms of self-condemnation and self-limitation.

But, now, you have erased the circle. Like the old song, you have come to the point of saying, "Don't fence me in!" As you erase the circle, you glimpse the Infinite. Your part was to erase the circle, removing old limitations to your prosperity. Now, you can move forward to unlimited goals.

THE INFINITE DOES NOT LIMIT US

The Infinite never limits us. "All is love and all is law," wrote Robert Browning. The Infinite is ready and willing to pour out to us all that we can accept. *That which you can conceive of, believe in, and confidently expect, must become your experience.* Remember, this is the law of life. Those of us who have had limited, unhappy experiences in this life are where we are because we have not really liked ourselves, we have not believed in ourselves and our own unlimited potential.

It is therefore up to us to change our habitual thinking about ourselves if we really want to change our experience. It is a proven fact that when we change our thinking about ourselves, we change our experience. The world will change, as far as we are concerned, to conform to our thinking. It is as simple as that.

WHAT, THEN, DOES LIMIT US?

The Infinite already is. We don't have to make it happen. We are one with the Infinite. Only our false concepts need to be changed.

Enlarge the place of thy tent, and let them stretch forth the curtains of thine habitations; spare not, lengthen thy cords, and strengthen thy stakes.

Isaiah 54:2

The tent is a temporary dwelling place. Each one must push back the borders of his temporary thinking. Limitation is not the Truth. We must not make it our permanent abode. We may have been mentally camping there, but it is not really for us. We must establish for ourselves a new expanded thinking, erasing that old self-imposed limitation that has fenced us in.

Jules Verne imagined a manned space craft being rocketed to the moon. Wernher von Braun and his friend, Hans Friedrich, conceived the same thing in mind and drew up workable plans for the execution of the idea. In 1952, Dr. von Braun, with the help of Dr. Friedrich and others, spelled out the entire project, with mathematical equations for each step necessary to the building of the rockets, the space platform and the lunar module, and the actual guide to the take-off, landing, and return. We are right on target at this time. Each step has taken place as planned in mind. Dr. von Braun and his associates enlarged the borders of their tents (consciousness) and the result of their expanded thinking is now manifest to all the world. Dr. Friedrich explained the whole project to me personally in 1953. That same year, Dr. von Braun and his associates set this all down in a paper which was published by the University of Illinois Press under the title "The Mars Project." This whole idea does not stop at the moon.

TWELVE FALLACIES REGARDING PROSPERITY

There are twelve common fallacies regarding prosperity that limit people, actually cut them off from prosperity. They are:

1. It is a fallacy to think that prosperity depends upon luck.
2. It is a fallacy to think that prosperity depends solely upon the ability to "get money."
3. It is a fallacy to think that money is evil.
4. It is a fallacy to think that it is wicked to be rich.
5. It is a fallacy to think that it is a virtue to be stingy.
6. It is a fallacy to think that the economic system is faulty and that therefore it is impossible to be prosperous.
7. It is a fallacy to think that the government will take it all

away in taxes and that therefore one can not prosper anyway.

8. It is a fallacy to think that prosperous living depends upon storing up goods or money for the future.
9. It is a fallacy to think that one is unworthy to receive.
10. It is a fallacy to think that there is virtue in poverty.
11. It is a fallacy to be a martyr, trying to prove that life is against one.
12. It is a fallacy to think that one has to be grim to be prosperous.

TAKE TIME TO TAKE A MENTAL INVENTORY

If you will give a little thought to the twelve fallacies listed above, honestly evaluating yourself, you will soon see that you have been giving mental houseroom to a few of them. You will find it well worth-while to make a list of some of your own self-imposed limitations. Where have you been selling yourself short? Where have you been limiting yourself, fencing yourself in?

You're the only one who's going to see this list, so be honest with yourself. There is something about writing things down that helps us to evaluate our thinking. Once you have made your list, open your mind to receive the Truth about yourself that will set you free from these limitations. It is never too late to make a fresh start. Many have found their true potential at eighty—yes, even in their nineties. Two of the most successful men I know were in prison for life when the Truth was revealed that set them free. Nothing can keep you in bondage except your own false thinking. Now we are starting on a new approach. Be prepared for some exciting discovery.

DOES PROSPERITY DEPEND UPON LUCK?

This universe in which we live is a universe of law and order. It is completely dependable. Since it is a universe of law and order we find that when we do certain things we are going to get certain results. How, then, could prosperity depend upon luck?

Prosperity does not depend upon luck. It depends upon our consciousness, the relationship that we have established with the Source of all Good. Prosperity depends upon our willingness to accept the Truth of Being and let it be applied in our daily living. Whenever there is a need in our lives, a vacuum is created and in comes the fulfilling of that need. *Before they call, I will answer.*[1] The Spirit within you knows you and your need, and is willing and able to supply that which is needed in your experience, according to your willingness to accept. Therefore, go forth in strength, letting your needs be known and opening your mind to receive. Do not hold back in letting your needs be known in consciousness. Think of them as already filled and they will be.

A man seems lucky. He discovers a uranium mine and sells his rights to it for twelve million dollars. Eight years later he is broke and actually in debt. Does prosperity depend upon luck?

A young man inherits three million dollars. How lucky can you be? Three years later he has wasted his fortune and become an alcoholic on skid row. Does prosperity depend upon luck?

No, prosperity does not depend upon luck.

DOES PROSPERITY DEPEND UPON YOUR ABILITY TO GET MONEY?

There are many people who believe that the only way they can be prosperous is to find ways and means of extracting money from other people. This fallacy implies a sense of separation from life itself, and such people spend all of their lives protecting what they have taken away from others. The

[1] Isaiah 65:24.

very thing that they have set up becomes the law for themselves. Life is not that way.

Seek ye first the kingdom of God (inner peace and divine order) *and his righteousness* (the right use of the Law) *and all these things shall be added unto you.* What things? Why, all things: food, shelter, clothing, and all that man needs.

Once we understand the law of life, that everything evolves in an orderly manner out of consciousness, we will not need to compete with others for our good. Our good does not depend upon another. It depends upon our use of the law. Why does one man prosper and another fail? Why do some companies become larger and larger while others fade quickly out of existence? It is all a matter of consciousness. The wise man builds a consciousness of prosperity.

The other day in an old file I ran across this excerpt of a sermon preached in 1889.

A man can't be hid. He may be a peddler in the mountains, but the world will find him out to make him a king of finance. He may be carrying cabbages from Long Island, when the world will demand that he shall run the railways of a continent. He may be a groceryman on the canal, when the country shall come to him and put him in his career of usefulness. So that there comes a time finally when all the green barrels of petroleum in the land suggest but two names and one great company.[2]

It is still true that if a man builds a better mousetrap the world will beat a path to his door. I believe that this saying evolved from the following quotation from the works of Emerson:

If a man has good corn, or wood, or boards, or pigs to sell, or can make better chairs or knives, crucibles, or church organs, than anybody else, you will find a broad, hard-beaten road to his house, though it be in a woods. And if a man knows the law,

[2] Dr. John Paxton, "He Could Not Be Hid." Sermon, August 25, 1889. *The New York Sun,* August 26, 1889.

people will find it out, though he live in a pine shanty, and resort to him. And if a man can pipe or sing, so as to wrap the prisoned soul in an elysium; or can paint landscape, and convey into oils and ochers all the enchantments of spring or autumn; or can liberate or intoxicate all people who hear him with delicious songs and verses, 'tis certain that the secret cannot be kept: the first witness tells it to a second, and men go by fives and tens and fifties to his door.[3]

Only the incompetent, only the man with a failure consciousness, thinks that he must take from another to insure his success.

IS MONEY EVIL?

Money is not a dirty word! It is not money that is evil. The Bible says that *the love of money is the root of all evil.* Money is the evidence of wealth, the symbol that we use for exchange. It is part of the circulatory activity of the Life Substance. Instead of bartering for things we need, we now use money to represent those things. So, if we say that money is evil, we are saying that clothes and food are evil, or the house we live in is evil.

No, it is not money that is evil, but loving money *too much,* putting it ahead of the Source of all good. The mistake is in making a god of money, worshiping money.

IS IT WICKED TO BE PROSPEROUS?

Perhaps prosperity has seemed wicked in some cases because of the way some rich men went about acquiring their riches at the expense of others. The Truth is that man can, through his own effort, produce into his own experience, through the working of his own consciousness, the good that he needs without having to deprive anyone else. History has proved that acquiring wealth does not depend upon educa-

---

[3] Emerson, *Journals of Ralph Waldo Emerson,* (Boston, 1909).

tion, family background, race or creed, but upon individual consciousness. The man who prospers helps himself and his fellow man and is in harmony with Life itself.

This brings to mind a great man, the late Dr. Frank Buchman who founded the Moral Rearmament movement. His work was always amply provided for. The resources placed at his disposal seemed to be unlimited. When someone asked Dr. Buchman, in a critical way, to explain this lavish display, he replied, "God is a millionaire!" I thought that this was a mighty good way to put it. He was one who did not limit the Infinite.

IS THERE ANY VIRTUE IN BEING STINGY OR POOR?

There are those who think that there is something spiritual about scorning money; that poverty and even stinginess is actually a virtue. I think that we can consider these supposed virtues together. Perhaps this fallacy was instilled in us by our pioneer forefathers who found it necessary to be quite frugal. We find that pioneering, whether it be two hundred years ago, or today, requires a certain amount of streamlining. We must pinpoint our desires and efforts so that we do not fritter away our directive energy. Thriftiness should not be confused with stinginess. Stinginess arises out of a belief in lack, a fear that lack is going to overtake us and that we must, therefore, hang on tightly to what we now have. When we are tempted to succumb to this fallacy, we should recognize it for what it is, that old enemy *fear*. No matter how much we gloss it over by feeling virtuous about it, it is based on a consciousness of lack and out of it will come more lack. There is virtue in using what we have, wisely; in investing what we have so that it will grow, but, there is no virtue in stinginess.

We have all heard people say, "I may not have much, but I'm proud!" The attitude that there is some virtue in being poor comes from the theory that this life experience is wicked and that the people who prosper in this life are going to have it all taken away from them in the next. Or, that by being poor in this experience, one can assure himself of being greatly rewarded in heaven. This is not true. Consciousness is the only reality, the only treasure we can lay up in heaven. Our consciousness is with us longer than we think. Eternity is a long time.

There is no virtue in poverty. People unwittingly say, "God didn't want me to have this nice house now." Don't believe it! It is not the Truth! Perhaps you didn't want it right then; perhaps that particular house was not for you. Perhaps there was something still better for you. Don't blame it on God. Don't fall into that old trap of blaming it on *the will of God.* The will of God for you must be in accord with the nature of God, Love poured out freely, infinite Abundance freely shared; therefore, the will of God must be for your highest, most acceptable good. The choice is yours. You can have all that you can accept in consciousness. There is no virtue in being poor.

IS IT IMPOSSIBLE TO PROSPER IN THE PRESENT ECONOMIC SYSTEM?

This one is as old as life. The ancient Romans blamed their failures on the same fallacy.

Fighting the economic system will get you nowhere. Whatever you resist is going to resist you. Through agreement we bring ourselves into alignment with Life. Love and prosperity go together. The Scrooges of this world may seem to prosper but, until they find love, they are the poorest of all.

The free enterprise system that we have in this country gives everyone ample opportunity to prosper according to his own consciousness of prosperity. We are talking about a law of life, and consciousness will prevail. Sooner or later, the man with a consciousness of prosperity will find himself in a position to prosper.

HOW ABOUT THE GOVERNMENT TAKING IT ALL AWAY FROM US IN TAXES?

When Peter asked Jesus what they were going to use for tribute money, Jesus told him to go down to the sea and throw in a line and pull in the first fish, and that in the mouth of the fish he would find the money for their taxes. This may seem like double talk to you. The Bible is a book of spiritual instruction. The fish represents an idea in the sea of Mind. The early Christians used the outline of a fish as their symbol. Jesus used this illustration to show that man was to reach down into the Universal Consciousness and take out of it an idea, whatever idea needed; that right within the idea would be the wherewithal to pay the taxes. So it is today. Right where we are is all that we need. The One Mind contains all that we need to draw forth that which is required to pay the taxes, or for any other purpose, providing we do not resist paying the taxes or other bills. People who struggle against taxes soon find that they end up having no income and thus no taxes to pay! As Jesus said another time, we are to render unto Caesar the things that are Caesar's and unto God the things that are God's. As we cease struggling and agree with Life, Life will supply all that we need and more.

BEWARE OF FALLING INTO SUBTLE TRAPS

Do you begin to see that each one of these fallacies is a subtle trap, a trap into which we have all fallen at one time or another? Our prosperity depends upon our ability to see through these subtle temptations, lifting our thinking above them.

No, prosperous living does not depend upon our ability to

store up money and goods for the future. Many found this out in 1929. Those who thought that because they had lost their savings life was over went down in defeat. Others went on to build new fortunes out of their own prosperity consciousness.

We can never be separated from our good. Prosperous living depends upon an absolute awareness that Life is infinite, flowing through our experience as we need it and when we need it.

ARE YOU WORTHY TO RECEIVE YOUR GOOD?

Some people do not believe that they are worthy to prosper. People have been offered great opportunities and have refused them because of a feeling of unworthiness. Some actually have a will to fail because of this deep-seated sense of unworthiness. Whatever we relate ourselves to, we become. Instead of thinking, "I am unworthy," start knowing, "I am an infinite being, the image and likeness of God. Life wants me to have the best. I am accepting the best. I am worthy of all good."

As a child of God, you can express prosperous living. As you demonstrate good, you are glorifying God. *All that the Father hath is thine.*

CAN LIFE REALLY BE AGAINST YOU?

Then there is that old martyr complex. The person who has to prove that life is against him. I suspect that all of us have been guilty of this one at times. Sometimes it is a subtle desire to punish the self because of some deep-rooted guilt. Sometimes it is a desire to punish another, to show that father or mother or wife is to blame for our suffering. The person who falls in this trap is unable to see his good when it comes and often refuses a good job or a good investment simply to prove that he is put upon or unfortunate. This is shutting the door in prosperity's face. Don't do it. Forgive and forget.

If you have thought of yourself as unworthy, start today to reverse the whole process. Start thinking of yourself as entitled to prosper and enjoy every good thing. You, too, can be prosperous through the right use of Self-Direction.

We have spent a long time discussing these fallacies because once they are understood and removed, we have removed many barriers to our prosperity.

Seeing through a fallacy of thought is the best way to erase it. It is only through erasing them that we can push out the boundaries of our own acceptance of prosperity. Therefore, I urge you, do not pass over these twelve fallacies lightly. Vow to be through with them once and for all; they are the enemies hidden within your own mental household.

When you have finished with them and are willing to let them go, go over again the five principles of building a prosperity consciousness.

1. *God's love is everywhere present and is not conditioned by person, place, thing, or circumstance.*
2. *Erase the circle—remove the limitations and let the Infinite live through you.*
3. *Man individualizes the Infinite by speaking His word.*
4. *That which you can conceive of, believe in, and receive must necessarily become your experience.*
5. *Give and Life gives back to you. Why? Because all Life is One.*

By now, you should be ready for principle number 5 which is the proving ground of all the rest—*give and life gives back to you! Prove me now herewith, sayeth the Lord of hosts, if I will not open you the windows of heaven, and pour you out a blessing, that there shall not be room enough to receive it.*[4]

Can you feel so certain that you are drawing from an Infinite Source that you are able to give freely of yourself and your substance? This is the test of spiritual wealth, the con-

4 Malachi 3:10.

sciousness of true prosperity. This is the proving ground where we put all we have learned into practice. Did you think it was by accident that Henry Ford, J. C. Penney, Andrew Carnegie, Robert La Tourneau, the Colgates, George Romney, Billy Casper, to mention a few, were so successful? You will find that they have all been great givers, tithing back into Life from 10 to 90 per cent of all that they earned. When we give freely we trust in the Source and thereby open our consciousness to receive freely.

A MEDITATION FOR TRUE WEALTH

True wealth is spiritual. It is a degree of spiritual consciousness, an inner security that comes from knowing the One Source of all good. True prosperity reflects an inner awareness of the Presence; it cannot be influenced by world conditions or man's opinion.

The Wisdom within is our supply, a never failing Source that goes with us wherever we go. *Lo, I am with you always, even unto the end of the world* (of illusion). Supply may seem to come from people. In truth, it does not depend upon any certain channel. If one door closes, another will open. Let us now stop limiting our supply. Know that it comes from an infinite Source.

KNOW FOR THE SELF:

The Wisdom within is my supply, a never ending Source of right inspiration, productive ideas, and guidance. I let this inspiration and guidance out-picture in my life as all that I need and more.

SELF-DIRECTION

I am prosperous. (Think this over a hundred times, if you have to, until it becomes embedded in your subconscious.) *I never entertain thoughts of poverty or lack.*

I am supplied from the Infinite Source with all that I need and to spare.

Right ideas come to me when I need them. I make right decisions at the right time.

I am never alone. I have a Silent Partner who works with me in everything that I do. He is right within me, working with me every moment of the day.

I have no regrets for the past, no fear for this moment nor any anxiety for the future. I am protected by an Infinite Power; I am guided by Divine Intelligence and I am sustained by a Loving Presence.

All is well and I am thankful.

**WHAT TO DO WHEN
THINGS GO WRONG**

This day we fashion Destiny, our web of Fate we spin.
WHITTIER "The Crisis"

THERE are times in each one's life when things seem to go
wrong; plans go awry, anticipated profits fail to materialize,
illness or accident breaks into the normal flow of daily activity. At such a time we all need something to fall back on, inner resources that we can count on.

The other day I listened to an interview of Kay Stevens
over the radio. Now, I do not know Kay Stevens but I'd like
to. She's the kind of a person we'd all like to know. I was very
interested in hearing her story. Kay Stevens is a singer. In the
interview, as I recall, she told of being on one of the lounge
programs in a big hotel in Las Vegas. She began to dream of
the day when she would be able to appear in the big room
where the big-time stars were. Each night after she had finished her program in the lounge she waited until the big
room was cleared and then she would go in and take her
place on the stage and sing. Her audience was made up of the
cleaning people and they seemed to enjoy it and so did she.
Each night her voice filled the big room. She visualized it full
of people. In her mind, she was the star of the program. Finally, her contract on the lounge program came to an end
and she returned to Los Angeles.

One night at fifteen minutes to six she received a telephone

call telling her to be at the same hotel in Las Vegas to take
over the entertainment in the big room at eight-thirty because Debbie Reynolds, the star of the program, was ill and
could not go on that evening. She answered, "I'll be there."
It was nearly six o'clock and she was in downtown Hollywood
when she received the call. It was nip and tuck from then on.
First, she called her hairdresser and asked him to meet her
at the airport; she called her home and told them to start
packing, that she would pick up her things at once; she made
arrangements to pick up her music and her accompanist. It
all had to be done at once. She got to the airport only to find
that all of the flights to Las Vegas had been cancelled because
of high winds in Las Vegas. She stood around with her little
party for a few moments. She did not say that she prayed but
I'll bet she did. She knew that somehow she was going to get
there and that is a prayer in itself. Bonanza Airline said that
they would put through a flight. They boarded the plane,
Kay still in her capris. Her luggage was there, she thought.
The hairdresser sat behind her and worked on her hair, and
then the stewardess informed her that none of her luggage
had been put on the plane because they could not have the
extra weight in trying to land at Las Vegas in the high wind.

She had no clothes, no music, her beautiful formal gown
was back at the airport; she had none of the things that she
had dreamed about as she pictured herself making her en-
trance in the big room. Surely things seemed to be going
wrong, but that didn't phase her. Immediately she reached
over and took one of the bags provided for airsick passengers,
pulled a pencil from her purse and started writing out a
program, thinking it through, all numbers that she knew and
could sing without music. They arrived at Las Vegas at about
eight-fifteen. A car with a police escort was waiting for her.
They rushed her to the hotel and right when she got to the
hotel they told her, "You're on!" There she was, curlers in
her hair, not dressed for the performance. What would you

have done? Kay is a trouper. Actually, she didn't have much to say about it. Her plans had been changed for her.

As I listened to the interview I couldn't help but think, *it's not what happens to us that matters, but how we react to it.* How do we meet life's adversities? Do we learn valuable lessons from our problems? Do they spur us on to new fields of unexplored activity? Best of all, do they help us build faith in God and in ourselves? I have an affirmation that I use when things seem to go wrong. It fits every situation.

> *There is no person, place, condition, or circumstance that can interfere with the perfect right action of God almighty within me right now.*

Kay Stevens knew that nothing was going to interfere with being her true self. She went right on, went over to the orchestra leader and said, "Here are my numbers," handing him the brown paper bag with her numbers written on it. They began the program. After a couple of numbers she sat down with the pianist and sang while he played and the hairdresser took the rollers out of her hair. One at a time she tossed the rollers out into the audience. She said that there were nine hundred people there and not one of them asked for their money back. Everybody was delighted. Why? It was different; it was unusual; it was the expression of her true self. The people fell into the spirit of the thing and cooperated. They loved her.

ALL THINGS WORK TOGETHER

All things work together for good to them that love God (good), said Paul. When we love the good within each other and within ourselves, we recognize the good as it comes into our experience. We recognize the good when another person is letting the spontaneity of life live through him. Every one cooperates, everything works together for good. Here was a performer who let life flow through her, accepting the change in plans with good grace, and everyone was pleased. In fact, the program was so well received that the management asked, "Can't you do it every show?" She was a hit because she did not panic, she did not let her ego get in the way. She flowed with life and life responded to her in a beautiful way. The very things that seem to go wrong can turn out to be blessings in disguise if we meet them in the right way.

A BLESSING OR A CURSE

Another man taught me this lesson in a different way. He was a man who had spent fifteen years in establishing a business. He had been hard working, diligent, persevering. And then, the freeway came along. He knew that the freeway was being built. He could not sell the business without disclosing all of the facts. When the freeway opened, he was no longer on the main thoroughfare and his business changed overnight. Where it had been flourishing one day, the next day there wasn't a single customer. He said to me, "What shall I do? Everything has gone wrong." He meant that his plans had gone awry.

"How did you make this business succeed in the first place?" I asked him.

"Well," he said, "I did it by using all of the ingenuity that I had. But, I've done this once. How can I do it all over again?"

"What would you say if someone came to you with this problem?" I asked him.

He thought for quite awhile and then he smiled. "Well," he said, "I can just hear you say in one of your lectures that we have to trust the Power within us to do the thing that has to be done, moment by moment. I remember that you gave us a little jingle. It went something like this: 'By the yard, life is hard, by the inch, life's a cinch.' I rather believe that if I start out trusting and knowing that there will be right answers, there will be. Suppose I do take a big loss in my business, it's only money. I still have my family, my health, and my awareness of the Power right where I am."

Maybe you think I wasn't thrilled to have him drawing these Truths out of himself like that. "Yes," I said, "you still have your ingenuity, your creativity, you can still express God's perfect Life right where you are and that's all that counts."

Every time things go wrong we have an opportunity to prove the Truth, to demonstrate the Power in our lives. Jesus was never at a loss when people came to him with their problems. The man who was blind from birth was healed and when the disciples asked him "who did sin, this man or his parents, that he should be born blind?" Jesus told them, *No one sinned, but that the works of God should be made manifest in him.* As we find in Deuteronomy: *the curse is turned into a blessing because the Lord thy God loved thee.*

My friend proved this. He started another business in another location using all the ingenuity and creativity he had. Today he is doing ten times better than before. The freeway turned out to be a blessing in disguise. It wouldn't have been, had he not met his problem in a positive, constructive way. He did not allow himself to become defeated to think that life was against him. *If Life be for us, who can be against us.* Life is always *for* us.

It really doesn't matter what caused the condition. If the barn is on fire, what difference does it make what started the fire. The question is, what shall we do to put the fire out?

THERE IS ALWAYS A WAY OUT

I love the story of two little frogs who fell into a pail of thick cream. One frog was filled with fear and had a deep sense of inferiority. He tried to swim in the thick cream but soon gave up. He choked on the cream and drowned. The other frog knew that he was going to get out of that pail somehow. He said to himself, as he looked over his shoulder at his drowning companion, "That is not going to happen to me!" So he placed his front feet against the edge of the pail and started to paddle with his long rear legs. In no time he had a pad of butter under him. As soon as he felt that solid island under his feet, he jumped out. He knew he could do it somehow and he did. He knew that there was a way out. He accepted the challenge and won. Again I say, *it is not what happens, but how we react to it that counts.*

DANIEL MET THE CHALLENGE

A classic example is the story of Daniel in the lion's den. Daniel had become very close to King Darius. Darius respected him and raised him up to a high position in his court. Only the king was above him. This made the other people in the court extremely jealous. They sought to trap Daniel. They got Darius to pass a law that anyone who worshipped any god other than King Darius would be punished by being put into a den of lions. Little did the king realize what he was doing to his good friend Daniel. He only knew that the people wanted to praise him, to worship him. This appealed to his ego. As soon as the law was in effect the jealous people began to watch Daniel and, sure enough, Daniel was worshipping his own God. The king had no alternative. He had to call his good friend in, even though he held him in high esteem, and send him to the lion's den. But, even as he gave the order, the king said, "Thy God whom thou servest continually, he will deliver thee." Then the king went to his palace and spent the night fasting. Early in the morning he went in haste to see how his friend was getting along. The Bible says that he cried with a lamentable voice unto Daniel:

"O Daniel, servant of the living God, is thy God, whom thou
servest continually, able to deliver thee from the lion?" The
king was overjoyed to hear Daniel say: "O King, live forever.
My God hath sent his angel, and hath shut the lion's mouths,
that they have not hurt me."

How would we feel if we were cast into a den of lions?
Could we trust enough, or would we say "I give up, everything has gone wrong for me." Daniel met the challenge just
as the king knew that he would. The angels in the Bible
represent divine Inspiration that comes to minister unto us.
No evil can befall us when we trust in the Perfect Power
within us.

YOU ARE THE MASTER OF YOUR FATE

Do you believe in fate? Do you believe that you are a pawn
in the game of life, doomed to failure no matter what you do?
Are you dissatisfied with the conditions in your life, but convinced that there is nothing that you can do about them?

This kind of thinking always reminds me of the story of
Bill and Mack, two construction workers who had their
lunch together every day. Each day at the stroke of twelve
they sat down together in the shade of the building project
and opened their lunch boxes. On Monday, Bill carefully un-
wrapped his sandwich. Picking up the top layer of bread, he
peeked inside.

"Peanut butter again!" he said with a look of disgust.

Mack went right on munching his own sandwich without
comment.

On Tuesday, Bill again examined his sandwich and with
even greater annoyance exclaimed: "Peanut butter again!"

Again Mack refrained from comment as Bill went ahead
and ate the sandwich.

On Wednesday, when the same routine was repeated, Mack

could no longer keep silent: "If you don't like peanut butter, why don't you tell your wife?" he said.

"Now, listen," replied Bill, "you leave my wife out of this. I make my own sandwiches!"

A little on the zany side, I'll admit, but sometimes a silly story points up the truth. I wonder how many of us are putting up with something we are fed up with, thinking that there is nothing we can do about it. What kind of "sandwiches" are we making for ourselves?

WHY DOES ONE MAN SUCCEED AND ANOTHER FAIL?

I go along with Emmet Fox:

> There is no such thing as luck. Nothing ever happens by chance. Everything, good or bad, that comes into your life is there as the result of unvarying, inescapable law. And the only operator of that law is none other than yourself. No one else has ever done you any harm of any kind, or ever could do so, however much it may seem that he did. Consciously or unconsciously you have yourself at some time or other produced every condition, desirable or undesirable, that you find in either your bodily health or your circumstances today. You, and you alone, ordered those goods; and now they are being delivered. And as long as you go on thinking wrongly about yourself and about life, the same sort of difficulties will continue to harass you. For every seed must inevitably bring forth after its own kind, and thought is the seed of destiny.[1]

Let's stop and think about this for a moment. What do you really believe about the problems in your life?

Why is one man sick and another man healthy? Why does one man live in a well-ordered, attractive home, while another is faced with the dismal surroundings of a slum?

[1] Emmet Fox, *Power Through Constructive Thinking,* (New York: Harper and Row, 1940).

Today, some are blaming these differences on racial discrimination but I know many people today who are of so-called minority races yet are making good salaries and enjoying the luxuries of life. If *some* can succeed, why cannot others?

Why is it that one man reaches the heights of popularity while another who has had the same background and advantages is despised and ignored? Have you ever wondered why so many good people are unhappy and frustrated? Why do many brilliant intellectuals have unhappy home lives and unsatisfactory personal relationships? If knowledge is power, why aren't all college graduates happy and successful? Today we are inclined to make a god of education. It becomes the *summum bonum,* the panacea for all ills. But is it? The truth is there are quite a number of uneducated or self-educated people who seem to have found the secret of successful and prosperous living while today some of our college people are unhappily protesting the very system that makes for equal opportunity for all.

ALL OF LIFE IS FOR YOU

Is there a secret? Yes! There is a law of life that says that everything we place before the mirror of life will be reflected back to us; that for every cause there is an effect; for every action a reaction; that every seed thought planted in the soil of life is going to bear fruit according to the kind of thought it is. Everything reproduces after its kind. Just as a carrot seed will not produce a radish, so a thought of failure will not produce success for us. That which we believe about ourselves determines our fate. The world continues to take us at our own evaluation; but, more than that, the law of life gives back to us with undeviating accuracy exactly what we believe we can attain, exactly what we are able to accept for ourselves in our own minds—no more, no less.

"All right," you say. "Suppose that is true. What am I going to do about it? I'll admit I've been defeated most of my life, thought that life and people were against me. Maybe I have planted wrong seeds. But, how am I going to dig them up and start over?"

Ah, that's the wonderful part about it! There *is* something you can do about it. You can start right today to create for yourself the kind of life you would really like to have. Nothing is against you. All of life is for you.

WE ARE NOT AT THE MERCY OF FATE

The thing is, so few of us really know ourselves and the important role we play in shaping our own destiny. The most important moment in one's entire life is that moment when he comes to realize that he is not at the mercy of fate, but that his thinking is the mold into which the substance of Life is continually being poured. The truth is that *that which we believe in, accept for ourselves, and confidently expect* is going to become our experience. It is the mold that we hold up for life to fill. It is an awesome challenge.

There are many ways of explaining this great law of life. It has been called the law of sowing and reaping; the law of cause and effect; and the law of attraction.

MENTAL EQUIVALENTS

Edison refused to accept failure. When he had failed some five thousand times to make the light bulb work, he said, when questioned about it: "We have discovered five thousand ways it won't work." As you know, he went on to success. Edison had the mental equivalent of success. He refused to accept failure. Mental equivalents are groups of thoughts which produce a thought atmosphere. "Every thought," said the great William James, "is motor in its consequence." The thought atmosphere draws to itself the action that gives it form.

If we have been setting up mental equivalents for disease and despair, poverty and failure, let's turn them around and put it all in reverse. Let's work on the idea that we are going to use positive mental equivalents which will take form as successful living. We make our own lives, but sometimes the mental images that we establish for ourselves are not representative of what we want to experience at all.

REPLACING FALSE IMAGES WITH GOOD IMAGES

How can we change the false images that we have been setting up for ourselves? It is really very simple. It just takes a little persistence to erase the old image and establish a new one. We do this very much as we would change the slide in a projector. It lies within our power to change the old image and replace it with a new image. For instance, where we have had an image of fear and anxiety, we can neutralize that image by establishing in mind a new positive attitude. Fear is based upon ignorance and ignorance will always yield to the light. Darkness cannot resist light. The light does not have to struggle with the darkness. When the light is turned on, the darkness just isn't. Just as there is no power in the darkness, so is there no power in ignorance. The moment we set up a new positive image of ourselves, the activity of life goes to work immediately to produce it for us. So, if we do not like the image we have had of ourselves, we can start right this moment to change it.

MIND HAS POWER OVER MATTER

Self-Direction is important for us to understand as a way of life. Once we are able to visualize the new concept in our minds, to accept it and believe in it, something happens in our experience and we find that we are able to leave behind us some of the failure patterns that we have longed to be rid of.

The whole theory is based on the assumption that the visible and the invisible are one and the same. Einstein, in the language of the scientist, said that energy and mass are equal and interchangeable. Thought, here, is the energy, and the effect of that thought becomes the mass or outer form appearing in our experience. Spinoza implied the same thing when he said that mind was not one thing and matter another. Phineas Parkhurst Quimby said: "Mind is matter in solution, and matter is Mind in form."

In other words, we are talking about the unity of life. Mind and matter are one; there is no matter for all is one, the visible and the invisible energy; the inner picture and the outer picture are one and the same. The outer reflects the inner. The outer, we might say, is the part of the inner that shows. "As within, so without," said Hermes. And someone else has said, "The body is the part of the soul that shows." Once we change the inner picture, the outer is bound to change because there is now no reason for it to continue. We have taken the power out of it. The outer cannot resist because it is only the reflection of the inner. Just as the slide in the projector determines the picture on the screen, so, too, the thought produces the outer effect in our experience. The outer is the shadow of the determining causation, that thought that produced it. Do you see what this means? We have the power to change the thought and thus change our experience. As we change the thought we set up a new mold for life to fill. The experience will follow, for it must reproduce the thought.

THE GREAT GIFT IS OURS TO USE

As the poet has said, we are the masters of our fate. The great gift is ours to use. The Power that we use through Self-Direction is not being meted out to us; it is already ours. If we believe that only a little good will come to us, then we are going to find that we will experience just a little good; for our experience will be only what we are able to accept for ourselves. It is like going down to the lake for water. Will we take a cup to be filled, or a bucket? The lake doesn't care; it is there for us. Likewise, if we believe that an abundance of good is available to us, we will find abundant good in every area of our experience. It is time we stopped railing at life and availed ourselves of the infinite good that is there for us.

Only a belief of separation from our good will keep the good that we desire away from us. The moment we entertain a mental image of separation, we cause ourselves to *be* separated from our good. Let us see how this works out. If we envy someone else his success, then, we are immediately setting up separation in our own minds because we are literally saying: "He is successful and I am a failure." In this way we put into mind a self-image of failure. Suppose we covet the possessions of another. Do we not again set up an image of lack? We are saying, in effect, "He has and I have not." When we resent the success of another we are lending emphasis to the idea of lack. By our very resentment we are establishing for ourselves the idea that we are not successful. The infinite supply is there, just as the lake is waiting to see if we will bring a cup or a bucket or a barrel to be filled. It is ready to pour itself out to us and provide all that we desire and more than we can even receive. It is we who have separated ourselves from this abundance.

To dwell upon old negative patterns is to bring more of their fruits into our experience. It is time we cast out the old thoughts of lack and failure and replaced them with mental equivalents of abundant success.

Let us agree together that from this moment forth we are through with negation, through with thoughts of inadequacy and failure. We are instead accepting our divine heritage; knowing that we are sons of the Most High dwelling in an atmosphere of Love where nothing is against us; where all of

Life is for us; where nothing is impossible to us; where nothing is too good to be true.

NOTHING CAN INTERFERE WITH THE PERFECT RIGHT ACTION WITHIN US

Things may seem to go wrong. Our plans may change, but nothing has gone wrong with the Spirit within us, nothing can happen to the Power that is right where we are. It makes no difference what may seem to happen, what may be man's opinion, there is only one Power and It is the same yesterday, today, and forever. Nothing can interfere with the perfect right action of God Almighty within us. When we stand firm in this knowing, conditions right themselves and the very things that seemed to go wrong turn out to be blessings in disguise. When things seem to go wrong it is only the challenge, the challenge to trust in the Power within us, around us, everywhere present.

Trust in the Lord with all thine heart; and lean not unto thine own understanding. In all thy ways acknowledge him, and he shall direct thy paths. Proverbs 3: 5, 6

Trust in the divine Law of Life with all your heart, your whole feeling nature, trust in the Law of infinite goodness and know that it will direct your path as you move through life from glory to glory, from one good experience to another.

SELF-DIRECTION

Nothing is against me. All of life is for me.
Every problem has an answer, an answer within me right now.
Whatever my difficulty I will find the blessing in it and emerge a better, stronger person.
Nothing defeats me because I know nothing defeats the Power within me.
Calling upon the Intelligence within me, I rechart my course for a more productive life.

XII BECOME THE MASTER OF TIME

Nothing is there to come, and nothing past,
But an eternal Now does always last.
ABRAHAM COWLEY

ARE you a slave to time? Did you wind your watch this morning? How many times have you looked at it since? "It's time to get up," you said. "It's time to eat breakfast. I must hurry and get to my office, so that I can hurry and get to my coffee break and hurry and get back in time to hurry out to lunch, and then I must hurry to get back for my next appointment," —and on and on. It is sad to relate, but we all seem to be pretty much in bondage to time these days. What is time? Who makes the rules about time?

YOU CAN BE THE MASTER OF TIME

Time is man's measure of eternity. All of the things that we take so much for granted about time are inventions of man's own thinking. They are purely relative. The subconscious mind takes no cognizance of time as we think of it. The time schedules that we allow to rule our days and nights are of our own making. In the Universal Subconscious Mind there is no time nor space. To understand how to use Self-Direction regarding time, we must understand that the subconscious mind is able to work in the area of the Absolute where there is no time-space relationship, nor time-space differentials. For time to be understood, we must realize that time depends upon space. Space is the measurement. It is through space that we are able to measure time; time is the interval that it takes for an object to move from one point in space to another point in space. This is what we think of as the time interval. The concepts of time and space are essential to each other, each is dependent upon the relative value of the other. Once we understand the truth about time, we come to see that we can become the masters of time.

HOW THE CONSCIOUS MIND USES TIME

The conscious mind is always reasoning and comparing according to human judgment. The conscious mind works on the relative level relating everything according to past experience. We continually relate one part of life to another, comparing according to our five senses. When we set up time schedules we are thinking of space relationships. We try to make these relationships conform to our desires. We are always shoving life around, trying to fit things into certain pigeonholes and grooves, trying to cause this and that to happen according to our time schedule as it relates to our concept of space. We limit ourselves by what our experience has been. The man who traveled by stagecoach across our continent would have no concept of the jet age. "Around the world in eighty days" was once a feat; but what has the space age done to our thinking? It now takes only a few hours to circle the globe—if you are an astronaut, that is. Yes, time is man's measure of eternity, man's concept, according to his experience, of how long it takes him to get from one place to another, or how long it takes him to get from one experience to another.

HOW THE SUBCONSCIOUS MIND USES TIME

The subconscious mind is not cognizant of time in the same way that the conscious mind is aware of it. The subcon-

scious mind follows the direction of the conscious mind completely and unquestioningly. It is the willing servant that
will wake us up in the morning at exactly the time we wish
to awaken. It is far more accurate than an alarm clock for it
does not look at the clock. And if we tell ourselves that we
are poor sleepers and awaken, "for some strange reason" at
three o'clock every night, that wonderful, obliging subconscious mind will see that we keep right on doing this, virtually shaking us awake every night at exactly three o'clock.
It has been said that "the subconscious mind has no sense of
humor" and those who have had this sleep experience know
that this is true. Whatever we consciously accept will be carefully carried out by that willing servant, the subconscious
mind. Self-Direction plays a very important role in our lives
when it comes to time. We find as we go along that the subconscious mind acts entirely upon our conscious direction.

WHAT HYPNOTISM TEACHES US ABOUT TIME

The psychology department at the University of Virginia
has provided us with some interesting experiments along
this line. A student was put under hypnosis and told that she
was to go back to the school where she had attended eighth
grade and was to walk to this school and then walk into each
classroom and look around. There were twenty classrooms in
the building. She was to walk the full length of the hall and
enter each classroom. To do this she would be allowed one
half hour. At the end of the half hour period she would be
asked to give a complete report on what took place. Moreover, she was told that she would have to allocate no more
than one and a half minutes to each classroom in this experiment because she would have to walk all the way through the
school to get to the end of the hall. She was to do this in her
mind while a metronome ticked away one minute at a time.
In her mind, under hypnosis, the girl did this. She went

through the entire process as directed, completing the whole assignment as planned except for one small item. The metronome was not ticking each minute—it was set to click each second, each second standing for one minute. In other words, the metronome clicked for thirty seconds.

At the end of thirty seconds the metronome was stopped and the psychology professor brought the young lady out of the hypnotic trance. She was then asked what she remembered. Step by step, she explained in detail what took place in each one of the rooms, what she had seen and remembered in her mind. She was amazed to find that the entire process had taken only thirty seconds instead of thirty minutes. The subconscious mind had adjusted immediately to her instructions.

You can row a boat across the lake and it will take a day or an hour. Whatever time you allocate, the subconscious mind will do it in that allocated time. You must first accept it consciously and then the subconscious will follow. There are so many examples of this in my own experience. If I say it will take me days to find some article in a store, that will be my experience; but if I say that it will all be done easily in less than an hour, somehow or other I am guided to the right place with no time wasted in the search. If I say, and this most negatively, that I probably won't have much time to write today, probably won't get started on the work until noon, the subconscious mind will oblige me by causing one delay after another to take place. As I sit down to my typewriter, I will note with a smile that it is exactly twelve o'clock and where did my morning for writing go?

On the other hand, if I give instructions to my subconscious mind that a certain job is to be finished at a certain time, trusting and knowing that through the invisible world of Mind it will be accomplished, it is as if I were lifted up on wings and in some effortless way the assignment is accomplished. It is done around the edges of my life so that when

I see the finished accomplishment, I am simply astounded. It seems like a miracle.

A SECOND EXPERIMENT

Another experiment at the University of Virginia was tried with a man in the class who had been a cotton farmer. He was put under hypnosis and in this state he was told that he was back on his farm and that he had an hour to go up and down all of the various rows of cotton and to count the bolls that were on the cotton plants. Asked if he could accomplish this mission in an hour, he said "I think that I can, I'm pretty fast." He was told that the metronome would click at each minute, or sixty times for the hour. Since the man had not been in on the first experiment, he did not know the trick that had been played on the first student.

Again the metronome was stepped up so that it marked every second instead of every minute. Mentally, the subject walked up and down the rows of cotton. At the end of the sixty seconds the metronome was stopped and the subject brought back to consciousness. Thinking that he had been working for an hour, he told them all about it. He had indeed covered the entire field, counting the cotton bolls on each plant.

We can see from these experiments that the subconscious mind does not judge time. It follows direction. When told that the metronome would click every minute, it accepted that, taking the order to cover the entire field. And so he did— in his mind. You see, in Mind there is no limitation in time or space.

You can imagine yourself standing on a street corner in New York City at 42nd Street and Broadway. In your mind, you can feel yourself having the experience of standing there, looking up at the tall buildings, looking down Broadway, noting the skyline, noting the crowds and the traffic. Immedi-

ately, you can change your thinking and be on the south rim
of the Grand Canyon. You can move from here to there and
because there is no time or space in Mind you have complete
freedom in your use of the one Mind.

WHAT OUR DREAMS TEACH US ABOUT THIS
CONCEPT OF TIME

Did you ever dream a long and involved dream just before
waking up in the morning, a dream wherein you seemed to
experience a lifetime of adventures, going from city to city,
meeting an endless stream of people from the past, struggling
through endless complications and confused situations, only
to wake up and realize that it all took place since the alarm
rang three minutes before? The dream seemed so real that
the memory of it lingered with you all day. You thought of
telling your family about it, but to relate it would take hours
and in your conscious state you did not have the time it would
take to go through it again.

All of this proves that our subconscious use of the Mind,
our point in the one Mind, knows no limitation of time and
space. It follows our direction as we mete it out.

THE ETERNAL NOW

The subconscious mind knows no past or future. It is always working in the present tense. It works in the Eternal
Now. In the book of Ecclesiastes we find this verse:

> *That which hath been is now; and that which is to be hath al-
> ready been; and God requireth that which is past.*
>
> Ecclesiastes 3:15

The subconscious mind, often called the subjective mind,
is completely subject to the conscious mind. It is really all

one mind, the individual use of the Universal pool of Mind. Normally, our use of the subconscious mind is subject to our use of the conscious mind.

Should you allow yourself to become hypnotized, your use of the subconscious mind would be temporarily subject to the conscious thinking of another. The word hypnotism is taken from the Greek word "hypnos" meaning sleep. In Greek mythology the God Hypnos was considered to be the god of sleep. Hypnotism is an artificial sleep induced by the hypnotist. The hypnotic sleep seems to have the appearance of sleep but it is a different kind of sleep. Through hypnotic tests we have been able to see the dual nature of the mind.

Your conscious mind reasons inductively, selecting from known experience and from various ideas that which it wishes to believe. The subconscious mind, on the other hand, knows only deductive reason. If you tell it that you wish to accomplish something at some time in the future, it will keep your desire "on ice" for you—always in the future. The direction that we give to the inner Self, our Self-Direction, should always be given in the now. The result, or the out-picturing of our direction may seem to come at a future date because the manifestation must necessarily be expressed in the relative, the world of relative time and space. In order to have our direction followed at all it must be given in the now, and it must be accepted now.

JESUS UNDERSTOOD THIS

I believe that this was one of the reasons why Jesus was so successful in the field of Self-Direction. He gave his commands to life not only in the present tense but with such authority that the results were instantaneous.

The Lord's Prayer, beloved by all Christians, is entirely in the present tense. It illustrates that the Infinite is right now being expressed in Its entirety.

Our Father which art in heaven, hallowed be Thy name.
Thy kingdom [is] come [now]. Thy will be done [now].

Jesus spoke his word and the manifestation appeared at once because he did not put a limitation on the use of Mind, nor did he feel that there must be a waiting period. He told the man with a withered arm "Stretch forth thine hand." The instruction was *now*. He did not say, "Your arm will get better as time goes on, perhaps, in time, you will be entirely healed." He accepted the man's wholeness then.

Remember the man who was blind since birth? When his sight had been restored, he said, "One thing I know, that whereas I was blind, *now* I see." There was no time lag because the direction was *now*. The healing had taken place immediately because Jesus knew that all of life was expressed at that very moment.

As we give directions to the subconscious mind, available to us at our point of use, let us remember that it is not aware of time or space. It is we who condition it. It is we who say, *there are yet four months and then cometh the harvest.* Remember, Jesus said, for they *(The fields) are white already to harvest.* It is we who say, "Someday I am going to take that trip," and then we wonder why it takes so long for our desires to become manifest. And then one day, in an easy way, we happen to give the direction in the *now*. We visualize ourselves as taking that trip. In our mind we walk through the door to that particular *Promised Land;* we plan our wardrobe, mentally pack, and choose our transportation. And, lo, it is done. Before we know it, we are taking the trip. The directions we give in the future tense are always alluringly dangled just beyond our grasp. The subconscious mind, our willing servant, thought we meant it that way. It knows only to follow our instruction. If we think it should take a long time to get well—to succeed—to find our life companion—to take that promised trip—then, so it will be in our experience.

Self-Direction is the answer, but remember, the subconscious mind is not bound by time or space. The time for miracles is *now! Thrust in thy sickle for the fields are already white unto harvest!*

SELF-DIRECTION

I now remove myself from the bondage of time. I take dominion over time by doing first things first. I direct the subconscious mind to do the thing at hand with ease and with certainty. I take all frenzy out of living by letting the Infinite live through me in an orderly fashion. I am not bound by the past nor limited by the future. I live now in the present.

XIII FOUR STEPS
TO A GOOD MEMORY

And when the stream
Which overflowed the soul was passed away,
A consciousness remained that it had left,
Deposited upon the silent shore
Of memory, images and precious thoughts,
That shall not die, and cannot be destroyed.
WILLIAM WORDSWORTH "Excursion"

I'LL NEVER forget Fuller Warren. Many years ago he made a real impression on me. I had just arrived at the University of Florida at Gainesville. It was a big moment in my life, that first day at the University. I was walking down University Avenue with two other fellows and we were all talking at once when a young fellow crossed over from the other side of the street, walked up to me and said,

"Hello, Jack Addington, how's everything in Jacksonville?"

"Fine, fine," I responded, wondering who in the world he was.

"I'm Fuller Warren," he quickly put me at ease. "I am from west Florida. I want to welcome you to the University of Florida. You have a brother named Dee and another named Rogers and a brother named Jim."

"Yes."

"Your father is in the construction business," he went on, as I nodded, my mouth hanging open by this time.

How did he know all this about me? How did he remember all of these details about an obscure freshman just starting his college career? He had made it a point to know about me. As a matter of fact, he made it a point to know about every man that went to the University of Florida during the time he was there. He knew everybody on campus.

Today, there is a bridge over the St. Johns River at Jacksonville called the Fuller Warren Bridge. Fuller Warren became the governor of the state of Florida and he might well have continued being governor for a long time except for the rule that a governor cannot succeed himself. He had a marvelous memory and I can't help but think it played a big part in his success.

Fuller Warren would meticulously take the names of each and every person who was coming to the university, find out everything he could about them; then, he would make a point of meeting them. He would find ways and means to do that. His memory was so precise that when he met you he would know what you were like and quite a bit about you.

Dick Drysdale, one of the young men who was with me that day, had been a reporter on the Jacksonville *Times-Union* before he went to college. Dick had met Fuller Warren about three years before when he had gone to the University of Florida to attend the state high school track meet. At that time, Fuller was attending high school at Blountstown, Florida. Three years later, they were both on a train going to a Florida–Georgia Tech football game at Atlanta, when Fuller stepped into a vestibule of the train and seeing Dick standing at the door, turned and said, "Why, hello, Dick, it's been three years since I've seen you." Dick didn't recognize him.

"I'm Fuller Warren," he said, "I met you over at the state track meet." Everything had a category with him. Everything had a place in his memory. He never considered any person or any circumstance too unimportant to remember.

How would you like to have just as good a memory as Fuller Warren? It is quite possible. He is endowed with the same mental computer you have—he just uses it better. Anything he can do, you can do, too, *if you use the same system.*

FOUR STEPS TO A GOOD MEMORY

1. Stop—Look—Listen

We remember what we want to remember. The person known for his good memory takes the time to stop and listen to a name when someone is introduced to him. He listens, and then he pictures it written out correctly, or even writes it down on a slip of paper so that it is engraved in his mind. A sloppy approach is generally responsible for what is called a poor memory.

2. The Learning Process Depends Upon Association of Ideas

The best way to memorize something is to associate one idea with another in sequence. All memory experts depend upon this system.

3. Trust Your Memory If You Wish It to Work for You

The ability to recall accurately requires confidence in the subsconscious mind. Trust your memory and it will respond to you to the degree that you yourself depend upon it. *That which you believe about yourself and confidently expect must become your experience.* This is the law.

4. Self-Direction is a Definite Act that Brings Definite Results

Your memory is only as good as the direction you give it. There must be nothing slipshod about your approach to it. You must be specific in directing your subconscious mind, definite in your direction, if you would have definite results.

PAY ATTENTION—GET A CLEAR IMPRESSION

Our memory rests on the things that we consider important. Is it important to you to remember names? If it is, you will stop and listen when someone is introduced to you. You will get the correct spelling of the person's name and picture it in your mind, or better yet, write it down so that you can have the added advantage of another sense perception. You are now introducing your eyes into the process. A pencil and notebook are essential tools of a good memory.

You have a good memory, you have a perfect memory. When people say that they have a poor memory, they simply mean that they are having trouble with their ability to recall. This is simply because they have not impressed clearly upon the mind the thing that they are desiring to recall. At the time, they did not consider it important enough to impress it clearly upon the mind.

Let's be honest with ourselves. How many times have we been introduced to a person and not even listened to the name because we don't care really whether we remember it or not; or we think that we won't remember it anyway, so why bother.

Suppose you meet someone named Mr. Cal Sudney. Now, how many people do you know named Cal Sudney? Not many, I warrant. Do you think to yourself, "I wonder how you spell it—oh well, I couldn't spell it anyway, so why bother —I won't bother to remember the name."

A few minutes later there he is again and you must introduce him to a friend of yours. Now, what is that guy's name, you think, some strange name—it came easy, I received it easily, but what was it? If you want to make a good memory impression, begin by making a sharp impression. Your memory is just like a tape recorder that is continually running, but you need to get a sharp impression on the tape. You must turn up the sound and tune it in properly or you will have just a jumbled playback that is no more in focus than your original impression.

If you want to remember someone's name, write it down. If you don't know how to spell it, ask him how to spell it. If you listen and impress the name upon your memory, rest assured it will be there when you need it.

You will always remember what is important to you—important enough for you to listen and consciously record it upon your memory. Stop floundering in the vague sea of confused responses. A sloppy approach is often at fault for what is called a poor memory. You will remember to the degree that you are interested. The tape recorder within you records according to the emphasis you put on something. If you are not interested in what is going on, you are going to have a very dull recording for that period. If you are interested, the recorder will make a deeper imprint and you will have a great ability to recall. Therefore, *stop—look—listen,* impress upon your mind accurately and clearly that which you wish to recall later.

ALL MEMORY EXPERTS DEPEND UPON THIS SYSTEM

There are people who make a specialty of giving memory courses. A memory expert can teach you how you can go into a room where there are forty or fifty people whom you have not met before. When you are ready to leave, you can stand at the door and shake hands with each one, confidently calling his name.

Just as a stunt, you may be given a sequence of fifty or sixty objects to remember and you will be surprised that you can remember them in sequence. The trick is in relating each one to the other. *The best way to memorize something is to associate one idea with another in sequence. All memory experts depend upon this system.* You can teach yourself the same process.

There are many people who would love to go on the stage but they think that they cannot memorize the lines. Anyone can memorize lines if they go about it right. It is a matter of establishing a sequence of thought, feeling, and mental pictures. The classic example used in remembering objects goes something like this:

Objects to be remembered are: ball, table, cat, wall, mouse, hole, tablecloth, pitcher, water, carpet. This sequence can be easily remembered if each is made to relate to the other. Picture the ball rolling across the table; it falls to the floor, the cat chases the ball to the wall, the cat then sees a mouse coming out of a hole; chases the mouse to the table and up the tablecloth; they knock over a pitcher filled with water; the water runs off the table and makes a spot on the carpet.

TRY PLAYING A GAME OF ASSOCIATION

All those who teach memory classes seem to agree that there is no such thing as a poor memory. What is called *for*getting, they say, is just *not*getting in the first place. The memory is like a muscle. A weak muscle is just a muscle that has not been developed by exercise. A so-called poor memory is just one that has not been exercised or trained.

Association has been found to be the very foundation of memory. In fact, without it there can be no memory at all. Every single thing that you remember—a name, a face, a line in a book—is the result of association on your part. The names, the faces, the quotations that you have not been able to remember are those for which it has not been easy for you to form associations in your mind.

If you would have a good memory you must form the habit of consciously forming associations in your mind. If you will place two or more names, or ideas, or thoughts in your mind at the same time you will find that it is much easier to remember them. Relate one thing to another, giving the direction to your subconscious mind at the same time.

For instance, Mary Fleetwood has big brown eyes and long blond hair. She looks like a Mary. Her husband, Frank Fleetwood is tall and looks like a runner, a person fleet of foot. I am going to remember Frank and Mary, brown eyed Mary and fleet-footed Frank. I am picturing them running through the wood—Frank and Mary Fleetwood. It doesn't take long, not as long as it takes to read this. It is all a flash picture in your mind, but be sure to repeat the names aloud and picture them with the picture of the people in your mind.

Be sure to get the thing you desire to remember right in the first place. Remember, practice does not make perfect, it only makes a habit. If you get the name wrong the first time, you are going to stumble over it each time you try to recall it. Get it right, impress it upon your mind, associate it with some idea or series of ideas in your mind, tell your subconscious mind that you wish to recall the information easily *and you will.* Try it, it's fun!

MEMORY ALSO STOREHOUSE OF FEELINGS

People who claim that it is impossible to memorize most likely were afraid to recite in school when they were children. Anyone can memorize unless he associates memory with the embarrassment of recitation in school or has some other block about it.

To the actor, memorizing is much more than just learning the lines; it is an association of words with feelings. He is not just remembering words, but is working on emotional response, trying to get into the mood, the spirit of the character. To him, learning the lines is not the most important part, he must speak the words with feeling. The memory is a storehouse of feelings as well as words.

You may think that you have a poor memory; that it is impossible for you to remember, but actually you remember everything that has ever happened to you. Sometimes, old feelings turn up after many years to give us trouble, some situation that has caused us to feel hostile, antagonistic, sorrowful, remorseful, or regretful. Something will remind us of an event long buried in the memory and all of a sudden we will feel depressed, anxious, troubled. Did you think that you could not remember? It is all there, everything that ever happened in your life, carefully preserved, waiting for something to call it forth.

It is impossible to erase the past from our memory, but we can make peace with it. That is where Self-Direction comes in. Just as we give the direction to the subconscious mind to remember something we would like to recall at will, we can also give the direction that heals some old hostility. We can replay in memory that past moment and then make peace with it; forgive, and neutralize the hurt until we surround that unhappy memory with different feelings, disarming it forever of any power to hurt us. It is all a matter of association, pictures, feelings, moods, and responses, all woven together with facts in the memory. How fortunate we are that we give the orders. Learn to place in your mind that which you would like to remember dictating the feelings and responses that you would like to have accompany the situation.

HAVE CONFIDENCE IN YOUR SUBCONSCIOUS MIND

You must trust the activity of the subconscious mind in order to have it work for you. Your ability to recall accurately depends upon the confidence you have in your memory.

If you tell your subconscious mind that you would like to awaken at six o'clock the next morning, you will awaken at exactly six o'clock *if you believe and trust the memory faculty within you* to remember and keep track of the time for you. The memory is like a computer, but like the computer, it requires direction. Suppose it is very important for you to make a certain long distance call. Because of the time differences in various parts of the country it is important that this call be made at exactly eight o'clock in the evening. How are you going to remember to do this?

I had this experience the other day. I thought of the call early in the morning and wrote on a piece of paper, "I will telephone Dorothy at eight o'clock this evening." I put the slip of paper in my pocket and promptly forgot all about it— or did I? I did not think about it during the day, but at eight o'clock, as I was finishing my dinner, the thought popped into my mind, "I will call Dorothy." I looked at my watch. It was exactly eight o'clock. I got up from the table and made the call. I had put the thought into my mental computer and it had followed through. There was no thought of "will I remember?" or "can I trust my memory?" I knew when I put it there that it would come through. We have to trust the subconscious mind as implicitly as the people at Western Electric trust the memory machine. Remembering is believing that we have that within us which can remember.

AGE HAS NOTHING TO DO WITH IT

We hear people say, "I don't have the memory I used to have." Many believe that they lose their memory as they grow older. Actually, memory does not depend upon youth. Age will not cause it to deteriorate. Anyone can develop a good memory. The memory is not a thing but an activity. It will be as active as you want it to be. It doesn't make any difference whether you are nine or ninety. No, you are not losing your touch. You have just been practicing forgetting instead of remembering. Start giving the direction to remember to your subconscious mind and *expect good results*. Start trusting your memory.

RELEASE IT AND IT WILL COME

If at first some name or some idea refuses to come through to you, do not be discouraged. This is not the time to condemn your memory. This is the time to trust it. The information is there. Give the direction, "I would like to recall this," and confidently wait for it to come through. Mentally walk away from it. Release it. Stop trying to remember. The easy touch is important here. Do something else for the moment. It won't be any time before the thing you desire to recall will pop into your mind. It works, but it depends upon the amount of trust you have in your memory.

> You can think and think
> And it comes to naught.
> When you think you're not thinking
> Up pops a thought.—Ginny Lenz

SELF-DIRECTION IS A DEFINITE ACT THAT BRINGS DEFINITE RESULTS

Perhaps if we understood how meticulous the mind is about recording everything we hear, or say, or think, we would have more confidence in our ability to recall at will the information we need.

In *The Law of Psychic Phenomena,* Thomson J. Hudson, M.D., tells of a man who had had a blow on the head rendering him unconscious. He was left on the street, later found and taken to a small hospital in the slums of London. He kept reciting a chapter from the Book of Isaiah which he quoted verbatim. This greatly interested the doctor in charge of the hospital who called a secretary to take down everything the man said. When the patient returned to consciousness, they asked him to repeat what he had said. He didn't know what they were talking about. Upon investigation it was found that this man had been down and out and had gone to a mission about a week before for a free meal. At the mission it was the custom to read from the scripture before feeding the men. So hungry had the man been that he had little else on his mind and so he had taken it all in, even though he wasn't aware of it. When the conscious mind was temporarily out of the way, the *recorder* within him gave back all that he had heard.

Another story reported by Dr. Hudson is that of a girl in her twenties who was involved in an accident. She, also, was taken in an unconscious state to a hospital where she began talking in a foreign language. The hospital authorities became interested and had someone come in and take down all that she said. It turned out that she was speaking Italian, but when she regained her conscious awareness she said that she knew nothing about Italian, could not, in fact, speak a word of it. At first, many thought that this was proof of reincarnation, that she was remembering Italian from some prior life. After probing further into the case, it was found that when she had been about eight years of age, she had had, for a period of one year, an Italian governess who normally spoke English in the household, but there were times when she would go off by herself and read aloud from Italian books and newspapers. At such times, the little girl would sit and listen to her. She had no idea what the governess was saying but was intrigued by the foreign language which made quite an impression upon her. The *recorder* within her mind took it all down and now, years later, she was able to recall it perfectly.

IT IS THE POWER TO RECALL THAT COUNTS

Your memory is perfect. Everything that has ever happened to you has been very carefully preserved. It is the power to recall that counts. It is not necessary to have the conscious mind out of the way in order to recall the past perfectly. It comes welling up in your thought when you least expect it. Go through your old papers and mementos. Perhaps you will come across an old diary that you wrote in your teens or a high school yearbook. Idly you leaf through the pages thinking at first that you do not remember the events; but soon you are recreating entire scenes. Back comes the memory of each event, the names come, one by one, and you feel yourself again in that wonderful, exciting time of life when each thing that happened was tremendously important.

THE THINK GADGET

I think and I think and I think that I think
While the little wheels whirr and the little lights blink;
There's a rattle, a humming, a rustle, a roar
And what do I get? What I got just before,
Some more thoughts to think . . . about doodles and dancers,
So I think some more thoughts that I think are the answers,
But the answers breed questions . . . They're fertile as rabbits,
And I moil and I toil and I fiddle and tinker,
And all that I get is a pain in my thinker.

So let me be still . . . oh, as still as a rock,
While I hear my heart beat like the click of a clock
And feel the blood flow like the pulse of the tide,
Then, I find that the answers are all waiting . . . inside.
Not words, noisy words, but a luminous glowing
The light in the shrine of the stillness of knowing.

Don Blanding

Stop telling yourself that you can't remember. You can remember anything that you want to remember. Young people who have difficulty remembering the assignment they study in school can remember with remarkable clarity a movie that they saw several years before on television. Most of us can remember the words of the songs we learned when we were young. Elderly people are accused of becoming senile when they start remembering only their youth, and that in great detail. The memory is good or they couldn't remember the past so clearly. If they fail to remember things in the present, it is because they have lost interest in the world of today.

There must be nothing slipshod about our approach to a clear memory. That which makes an impression upon us will be easy to recall. If we pay attention, giving definite direction to the subconscious mind, we can remember anything that we would like to remember. At any age, we can have what is called a good memory, the ability to recall at will information that is there waiting for us to call it forth.

SELF-DIRECTION

I trust my subconscious mind to remember. I release that which seems to elude me, and trust my subconscious mind to give me the answer I seek.

XIV RELAXATION WITHOUT TRANQUILIZERS

I count only the hours that are serene.
MAURICE MAETERLINCK

MARK TWAIN once remarked that everybody talks about the weather but nobody does anything about it. So it is with relaxation. We hear a lot about relaxation. Everyone feels the need of it but few do anything about it. Many of the television commercials today have to do with relaxation or getting rid of tension. If one was to believe the commercials, he would soon conclude that tension headaches were such a necessary evil that each one of us should be armed at all times with medication to combat this menace.

WHERE IS RELAXATION TODAY?

The woman of my mother's day got her housework done in the morning and took a nap after lunch. Then, bathed and fresh in a clean, starched dress, she sat on the porch, her hands in her lap and relaxed until time to prepare dinner. Today, with all our labor-saving devices, why aren't we more relaxed? Let's take a look at some of the things we do to relax.

People today are pursuing all kinds of activities supposed to bring relaxation. But, do they? Is it relaxing to become emotionally involved in bridge, football, baseball, and golf? Take the person who goes to a football game to relax. His team has got to win! The game becomes close. He sits on the edge of his seat. His frustration increases. He wants so much to win, but there's nothing he can do about it except shout himself hoarse. He becomes more and more tense. At the end of the game, he's a nervous wreck.

And how about that weekly golf game. "Now I know what's wrong with my game!" you tell yourself. All week long you've mentally analyzed your swing, your stance, the shots you missed last week. This time you're going to make it, this time you're going to lower your handicap, start shooting in the eighties. But somehow it doesn't go as well on the course as you thought it would. Perhaps you're trying too hard. You become tense and upset over a few missed shots, your score is shot for that day and you are apt to go home more tense than ever.

Come Sunday afternoon, you take the family out for a ride on the freeway. Happy days are here again! What a way to relax! Everybody else had the same idea, but there isn't a relaxed face in a carload.

Of course, there is nothing better for relaxation than a good night's sleep—or is there? Most people go to bed at night tense and wake up more tense. Before you can wake up relaxed, you have to go to sleep relaxed. Thinking that just going to bed and sleeping through the night will relieve tension is a fallacy. If you go to bed tense, you will sleep tense. It is important to learn to relax if one would enjoy relaxed sleep.

I know a New Yorker who imports furniture from Europe. Up until a few years ago he made three buying trips each year. He used to go by ship and then travel around Europe on the train. He told me that each trip took about a month. He looked forward to those trips, he said, because he was more relaxed when he returned than when he left. The time spent aboard ship he found quiet and relaxing. He relaxed on the train. There was nothing else to do. Now, he goes by jet. He gets there in a few hours. Does he take this "saved" time to go somewhere and relax? No, he uses it to make more calls in Europe. He sets up new outlets in the United States. He is ten times busier with the time-saving travel methods of today than he was before. He takes tranquilizers to become relaxed; then he needs "pep pills" to keep going! What a life! He told me the other day that he didn't know how much longer he could stand the rat race. "I feel as if my soul never has a chance to catch up with my body," he said.

Exhausted after a tense day at the office, many people rush to a bar or hurry home to wrap themselves around a couple of drinks, thinking that this will relax them. It seems relaxing. But, liquor is a stimulant. It first stimulates and then stupifies. When the effect wears off, one is more tense than ever. Liquor does not relax anyone.

WHY IS IT NECESSARY TO RELAX?

Dr. Hans Selye of Montreal has stated that every disease is the result of stress. More and more people are coming to accept this theory.

It is only when we are relaxed and at peace within ourselves that we are able to meditate, to commune with the inner Intelligence that provides us with fresh ideas. It is impossible to be truly creative when we are tense and nervous. When one is tense, he works at a greatly reduced level of efficiency.

One of the most important things in life, whether you are an athlete, an actor, a musician, or in any other field, is timing. Timing depends on relaxation. Right timing is relaxing in action. The first thing any great coach teaches his athletes is timing. Timing and relaxation go hand in hand. The golfer who hits the longest shots has the most relaxed swing. Note the swing in slow motion of Billy Casper, Arnold Palmer, or Sam Snead. The golfer's prayer is: *Lord, give me the strength to hit it easy.* Through relaxation we learn to conserve our energy, releasing it at the right time, giving it real focus and purpose.

Tension of itself is not an evil thing. It is constant tension that is dangerous. Life is a continual ebb and flow. There is a time to act and a time not to act, a time to tense and be ready to spring and a time to relax and release all tension. Watch the reactions of a cat. Could anything be more relaxed than a cat? But, the next moment it is tense, poised, ready to spring. When it springs it uses all of the energy stored up during its period of relaxation. We must take a lesson from the cat if we would take dominion of our lives.

PEACE IS NOT PASSIVE, BUT ACTIVE

It is a fallacy to hold that peace must be passive. Peace is mental and spiritual activity which is centered and controlled. At the center of the wheel is the axis. When the wheel and the hub are in perfect balance, the axis seems to be completely still, yet, it really is the center of the power. All of the action stems from this one point. The eye at the center of the hurricane is a center of peace, but fraught with power.

I know a man who buys and sells stock on the floor of the New York Stock Exchange. He completes hundreds of important transactions every day. All around him appears to be bedlam, complete and total confusion. He pauses many times during the day and thinks to himself, "I am centered in peace. Peace fills my whole being. I am calm, serene, and tranquil. My mind rests in peace." All during the day he is the picture of poise. Not only does he appear poised, but he is truly inwardly poised. He is never harried nor hurried. He keeps his "cool."

A person who is poised flows with life. He has no resistance to life, no fear of life, no contention with life.

DISPELLING CHAOS AND CONFUSION

We all get caught up in the confusion that results from whirling around too fast on that outer rim of life. Then, we need to go within, to become still and contemplate that inner peace that is never confused, never in a hurry, never disturbed. It is the truth of our being. It only awaits our recognition of it.

Nothing can separate us from this peace that is within us *unless we let it.* It is only our responses to life that get us into trouble. The real Self abides in eternal harmony. It is possible to dwell in that harmony at all times by turning away from the thought of confusion, by refusing to fear things and conditions in the outer world.

RELAXATION STARTS WITH MENTAL POISE

It is possible to remain poised and calm, no matter what happens. Lily Pons, famous opera singer and wife of Andre Kostalanetz, once remarked, "If a fairy godmother could endow each of us with the quality we value most—and which we think would make living a joy—my choice would be poise." Poise enables us to move serenely and self-confidently in our world, no matter what alarms, shocks, or changes we experience. If you lack poise, every chance wind buffets you; the unexpected, instead of adding color and zest to your life, wears you down with worry.

Lily Pons tells of an experience she once had in Hawaii where, when she came out on the stage, the audience burst into laughter. Now, this was a challenge to even the staunchest. Perhaps the thing that all stage personalities fear most is to be laughed at, to be ridiculed. Lily Pons wondered why they were laughing. She had looked in the mirror just before she came on stage so she knew it was not her appearance. With complete poise, she smiled in a friendly fashion and took a quick glance around. She saw a sign above her which said "Wrestling Tonight." Holding up her hand, she said with great presence of mind, "Ladies and gentlemen, the first number I will wrestle with is . . . ," naming her aria. The audience applauded, the laughter stopped. She went on with her concert. A bit of humor saved the day.

PEACE IS AN INSIDE JOB

Peace of mind and inner poise is not something that can be wrapped around us by another. It comes from within. The late Don Blanding wrote a book entitled *Joy Is an Inside Job*.[1] So it is with peace. There is an old saying, "The wise man looks inside his heart and finds eternal peace."

"Nothing can bring you peace but yourself, nothing but the triumph of principles," said Emerson. "In quietness and confidence shall be your strength," said the prophet Isaiah. Our security is of God. It is an inner condition that is not affected by outer circumstances. God within is peace, the eternal peace of the spheres.

Make up your mind right now that you are going to develop inner poise; that you choose to react to every situation with poise. Think of the clock that ticks relentlessly on, the same even rhythm, tick-tock, tick-tock, tick-tock. Nothing disturbs the clock. It does not react to the noise of the street, the roaring of trucks and sports cars, the screaming of sirens, the jets overhead. Robert Louis Stevenson wrote, "Quiet minds cannot be perplexed or frightened, but go on in fortune or misfortune at their own private pace, like a clock during a thunderstorm."

It was Milton who said, "The mind is its own place, and in itself can make a heaven of hell, a hell of heaven." There is nothing so valuable as a quiet mind.

"It all sounds wonderful," you may say, "but how can I

[1] Don Blanding, *Joy Is an Inside Job*, (New York: Dodd Mead & Co., 1953).

stop worrying? How can I turn off my mind and make it stop going around in circles like a squirrel in a cage?"

ESTABLISH REACTION IN ADVANCE

There are times when we all are tempted to lose our poise. It is important to establish in mind, in advance, what our reaction is going to be at such times. Those who pride themselves upon "going to pieces" will go to pieces at the drop of a hat. Those who talk about chaos, will experience chaos often and regularly; but those who are centered in peace will calmly declare, "This does not move me; I am profoundly undisturbed."

PSYCHOGENESIS AND RELAXATION

Through Psychogenesis, we know that everything begins in mind. Relaxation, tension, peace, and poise are all states of mind. The conscious mind sets the tone and the subconscious mind follows it with precision. Put your hand up behind your head—hold up your index finger and move it from side to side. You don't see this action taking place but you know that it is there. How do you know it? You know, from experience, that you can give orders to the various parts of your body and they will obey you. When you told your finger to move from side to side, you took dominion over that finger. The finger did not answer you back and say, "I am tired. I am tense. I cannot obey you." Nor, did you expect it to. The same thing applies to every part of your mind and your body. They will obey you *if you take dominion*. Mental and physical relaxation is simply a matter of taking dominion of the situation.

THE BODY IS LIKE A SYMPHONY ORCHESTRA

The body can be likened to a symphony orchestra. You are the conductor. Every instrument must be synchronized with the whole orchestra. The exercise that I am going to give you now will help you synchronize the various parts of your body into a relaxed whole.

The conductor of the symphony orchestra has only to raise his baton and the entire orchestra becomes poised and ready to follow his direction. One movement of his baton and the entire group joins together in perfect harmony. Like the conductor, if you will practice this exercise regularly, there will come a time when you will give the command "I am relaxed," and every part of the body will follow your directions and you will instantaneously be relaxed.

AN EFFECTIVE RELAXING EXERCISE

I am relaxed. Every muscle, every cell, every atom of my body is relaxed. I am taking dominion and giving the following orders to my body:

My toes are relaxed (flex the toes, tense them, turn them up toward the head and then consciously release and relax them).

My feet are relaxed (tense the feet and then consciously relax them).

My ankles are relaxed (tense the ankles and then consciously relax them).

My knees are relaxed (tense the knees and then consciously relax them.)

My thighs are relaxed (tense the thighs and then consciously relax them).

My hips are relaxed (tense the hips and then consciously relax them).

My fingers are relaxed (tense the fingers and then consciously relax them).

My hands are relaxed (tense the hands and then consciously relax them).

My arms are relaxed (tense the arms and then consciously relax them).

My diaphragm is relaxed (tense the diaphragm and then consciously relax it).

Now I am letting my shoulders relax, letting go of any burden I have been carrying. I am relaxing my neck muscles (tense them then relax them). I am relaxed. My scalp is relaxed . . . my head is relaxed . . . my brain is relaxed . . . my mind is relaxed . . . my eyes are relaxed . . . my face is relaxed (let expression go limp) . . . my whole body is relaxed. Now in this relaxed state, I surrender myself to the Perfect Power within me. I realize that all of life continues without my doing anything about it . . . *I am letting go and letting God!*

The ability to relax is so important that I am going to give you another exercise. The Self-Direction exercise is more compact than the other. You will note that in each of the exercises the first person "I" is used. You are giving the direction to the subconscious self within. Remember, too, that the more often these exercises are repeated, the more they will become a part of your habitual thinking. You will begin to think habitually of relaxation, rather than pressure and strain.

SELF-DIRECTION

I am completely, perfectly, and wholly relaxed. I am letting go right now of every muscle, every nerve, every bone, every tissue in my body. I rest in the knowledge that there is within me an Intelligence which knows how to make my body function perfectly, which knows how to make my affairs function perfectly, which knows how to make my life function perfectly. I let the Intelligence within me tell me what to do and how to do it. I move easily through life, doing the right thing at ex-

actly the right time. I am free from any irritation. I am in perfect harmony with life. Nothing irritates me. No person annoys me. I do not condemn myself. I have no anxiety for the future. I surrender my every action; my every demand; my every fear, worry, anxiety, and burden to the Perfect Power within me. I am completely relaxed.

XV   STOP WORRYING
AND START LIVING

Attempt the end and never stand to doubt;
Nothing's so hard, but search will find it out.
ROBERT HERRICK

Let's take a look at that old bug-a-boo, worry. I suppose most of us worry now and then. We all know people who worry too much. Many of us would like to stop worrying for the sake of our health and happiness—not to mention the health and happiness of the rest of the family!

GETTING OVER THE WORRY HABIT

The other day I heard about a compulsive worrier. A man came from San Francisco to see me, a nice looking, well-groomed man who came right to the point. He needed help because his wife worried too much. He said that it had come to the point where he couldn't take it much longer. And then he started enumerating some of his wife's worries. She worried, he said, about her health; about his health; about his business; about their lack of money; about the money that they do have; about their married children; about the world situation; about everything. From what he said, I could see that she was just about the most efficient, world-wide, champion worrier of all time.

He told me that for many years he had been trying to make everything right for her so that she would not have to worry.

Finally, it dawned on him that this thing was deeper than the apparent object of the worry. If there wasn't something obvious to worry about she'd find it anyway. He said this new insight came to him one day when he had refused to worry with her about some trivial thing. He could see that this continual worry pattern was having a detrimental effect on her health. Things had really gotten out of hand. He had come to see me because he realized that something had to be done.

Well, there are times when we all get caught up in excessive worry. This is a common problem. Are there any two words that strike up more resistance in a person's mind than the words "stop worrying"? Yet, that is exactly what we have to learn to do. To stop worrying we have to learn to take our attention away from the object of our worry, or change our attitude toward the object of our worry. It really doesn't help us at all for someone to tell us to stop worrying. It only serves to further frustrate us.

WHAT IS WORRY?

What is worry? Worry is a thin trickle of fear that runs through the mind, the longer it is allowed to run, the deeper the groove it cuts. If we worry long enough and expertly enough, we finally succeed in working up a good anxiety neurosis.

I ask you, what has worry ever produced in your life? Have you ever found worry to be of benefit to you? Worry has never accomplished anything. We worry rather than face up to our problems constructively. There is no more futile activity than worry. We all know this, and yet, we are all guilty.

WORRY IS CUL-DE-SAC THINKING

As I sat down in my plane seat and fastened my safety belt, I heard a voice, "Dr. Addington, you are just the man I want to talk to. I am on my way to Los Angeles and I have to make some decisions and make them quick. Will you help me?" I told him that I would do what I could do, but he would have to make up his own mind and arrive at his own decisions. He said that he understood this . . . and then started telling me his troubles. I volunteered several suggestions, and to each one he started his objection with, "Yes . . . but. . . ." Each one of my suggestions were simple, direct, and workable. Each time he objected with his "Yes . . . but," he seemed to get a broader grin on his face, as if to say, "See, I've got you stumped, too." Finally, I ran out of suggestions. He sat there with a kind of smug look, as if to say, "My problems are really something, aren't they?"

All of a sudden, it struck me. He was not looking for answers, he was looking for objections. He was engaging in cul-de-sac thinking. This is where every line of thought runs into a blind alley. The rich young man who came to Jesus and asked what good thing should he do to have eternal life, was told that he should keep the commandments. To which he replied, "Which?" Then Jesus enumerated the commandments, one at a time. "Yes, but," he replied, "I have kept them all from my youth up." Then Jesus told him to go and sell all that he had and give the money to the poor and then come and follow him. When the young man heard this, he went away sorrowing, for he had great possessions. I suppose in his mind he was saying, "Yes, but I can't do that. He must not realize how much wealth I really have." This young man was not looking for answers, he was looking for objections, and finding them.

Another form of cul-de-sac thinking is "What if . . . ?" What if I don't get the job? What if I get sick and have to stop working? What if I fail? What if the marriage doesn't work out? There are so many "what ifs" and all of them equally futile. Let's be done with cul-de-sac thinking. It is like getting ourselves down in the trap of a dead-end street and then bouncing against the railing there.

Let's stop trying to prove that we have big problems. The way out of cul-de-sac thinking is the transforming of the mind. Know that Mind has all the answers. Know that there is a way out of every difficulty. Know that with Mind all things are possible. There are no impossible situations when we let the Universal Mind guide and direct our lives. It provides not only the answers but the way in which the answers will become manifest as good experiences in our lives.

WORRY IS NEGATIVE USE OF IMAGINATION

We can use the imagining faculty of the mind for constructive or destructive purposes. When we imagine the worst happening, then that is worry and it is destructive. True, the things that we worry about seldom happen; but worry itself does us as much harm sometimes as if they did. Positive thinking is the gateway to right and perfect action. Negative thinking blocks the free flow of the creative processes of the mind. Worry is contagious and can contaminate all who come within its range; that is, if they let it in. Fortunately, one can become immune to worry as one becomes immune to disease.

HOW TO DEAL WITH WORRY

Do you realize that you cannot think about two things at one time? Sometimes we think so fast that it may seem as if we entertained more than one thought at a time, but actually only one thought can occupy the attention at one time. We may entertain a hundred and fifty ideas, or thoughts, in a minute, but in each one of those fractions of a second we are thinking only one thought. Therefore, when we allow ourselves to think a worry thought, we are excluding a faith thought filled with Power.

Now, you know, and I know that worry is a basic cause of many physical ills; that worry causes us to have negative reactions to life completely antagonistic to our deepest desires. Worry is a troublemaker in every respect. The first step in overcoming worry is to admit right off that worry never accomplishes anything; that it is harmful to the worrier; that it is blocking the fulfilling of our highest desires; that it will have long-range negative effects in our experience. Once we admit these facts, we begin to see that we really don't want to have anything to do with the worry habit.

We are not at the mercy of worry thought patterns. There is something that we can do about it. Start out by looking worry right in the face and telling it: "I am not afraid of you. You are nothing trying to be something!"

THE FOUR MOST COMMON WORRIES

Sometimes it helps to take a look at some of our favorite worries and see if we really need to spend so much time on them after all.

1. The worry that there won't be enough money to take care of our needs tomorrow. (Somehow or other we always manage to survive today.)
2. The worry that there won't be physical health in the future.
3. The worry that there won't be good mental health.
4. The worry that we will be left alone, rejected and neglected, without love and companionship.

You will note that all four of these worries have to do with taking anxious thought about tomorrow. With just a little thought we can see that the things that we worry about in these four areas rarely happen. We waste our energies worrying when we could be putting them to work constructively.

Take, for instance, that worry about our money running out. Some people actually think that worrying about money is a necessary activity of the mind, that if they don't worry about their money they will end up losing it. Others believe that worry goes with being frugal and is the only way to see that there is enough for the future. They think that the big idea is to worry now, so that they won't have to worry in the future.

The interesting thing is that once the pattern is set for worry, the object of the worry ceases to be important. There is always something to worry about even if we have to lift every stone to find it. Once we have developed that old worry habit, we have no trouble at all finding an object for worry.

I am reminded of a young couple. The wife worried and stewed from morning until night. She worried out loud constantly. When she was quiet her husband would laughingly ask her, "Millie, are you planning your next worries?"

The other day I overheard a conversation between two women. One woman remarked that she felt guilty most of the time. She said that she felt guilty about a great many things, but she didn't mind because it made her feel virtuous to feel guilty. Her friend topped that remark when she answered: "I worry all the time, but I don't mind because when I worry a lot, I smoke a lot, and when I smoke a lot, it keeps me thin." Well, that's one way to look at it.

You may wonder why I'm going into so many negative aspects here, but I find that it helps to see just how foolish worry really is. The first step in overcoming the worry habit is to make up one's mind to be through with it. Just as when a smoker decides to quit the habit or an alcoholic makes up his mind to stop drinking, the first step is: "I do not choose to waste my time any longer worrying." Like giving up any bad habit, we have to be willing to release it. Just as we would remove a plate from the table and place it on the kitchen counter, we must take the worry and place it in the "do not touch" file.

HOW ONE PERSON OVERCAME THE WORRY HABIT

Here is how one woman told me she overcame the worry habit. She met it so effectively that it changed her entire approach to life. She said that it didn't matter what she was tempted to worry about, she had three little words that took care of the matter: "God is there."

If she was tempted to worry about money, she reminded herself, "God is there. Infinite Abundance is there. The Wisdom and Intelligence to know what to do at the right and perfect time is there. God is the Source of infinite Abundance. If there are any steps that I should take, divine Intelligence knows what to do and guides me into perfect right action. God is the Source of all of the ideas that I could ever need and God is there. I need not worry."

If she was tempted to worry about health, she gave herself the same spiritual *medicine*—God is there. To her, this statement meant: "God's perfect Life is right where I am. In Spirit I live and move and have my being. God lives through me and I am whole. I need not fear."

She called these little capsule prayers *spot treatments*. She said it worked. She broke up the pattern of worry from then on. She told me that it came to her one day that to worry was to deny God; to mentally argue that God was not able to take care of her; that every moment spent in worry was a moment lost, a moment that could have been spent recognizing the Presence. To deny the Presence was, she said, not only foolish on her part, cutting her off from all Good, but was dishonoring the Author of all Good. On the contrary, she said, that through scientific prayer she had been able to put God first, relying entirely upon Him, knowing that His perfect Life, Omnipresent, Omnipotent, All-knowing, was divine right action in every part of her life. Trusting in the Omnipresence, she knew that all was well, not only for today but for the future. Once she had established this thinking pattern it ruled out worry. It was impossible to worry and trust at the same time.

WORRY IS NOT THE ANSWER

It makes no difference what the appearance may be. A person may be down to his last nickel, alone, unloved and desolate. Worry is not the answer. To turn to the Power to which all things are possible is to transcend the problem. As one rises above it, he is able not only to meet the need of the moment, but to step out into a greater dimension of livingness. It takes a little doing to overcome worry, but there are extra blessings—fringe benefits, you might say—each time we make the effort to realize *God is there.*

THREE GOOD WAYS TO STOP WORRYING
AND START LIVING

In a nutshell, there are three good ways to stop worrying:
1. Realize God is there.
2. Practice being a positive thinker.
3. Take positive action after praying for guidance.

Carry on a conversation with yourself something like this:
"I believe that right action is taking place in my life.
"I believe that God's perfect Life lives through me.
"I believe in the Power of God in my life."

Remember that your thought is providing the mold for the shape of your future life. That which we think about today are the *work orders* that we are giving to our subconscious minds and the creative process goes to work to bring them into form. The tendency our thought is taking is important. Do not blame yourself for past wrong thinking, but start today to keep your conversation in heaven. When you are tempted to worry, talk to God, not about your problems, but about that which you would really like to have come to pass.

Don't overlook step number three. If there is something to be done, some constructive action to be taken, do it fearlessly. Many people sit around and stew about something that needs to be done.

Do it! Make that telephone call that you have been dreading. Make that decision you haven't wanted to face. Go and see that friend you have been worrying about. Write that term paper you have been putting off. Call the client you have dreaded seeing. Most people spend many hours in negative preparation, going over and over in their minds a sort of nightmarish dress rehearsal of the dreaded step to be taken. Again and again they struggle through an imaginary situation in which they find themselves lacking. How much better to draw upon the Power within and step boldly forth and make it past history. Nothing is ever gained by advance worry. Start a new program of *do it now*. You will find that it is a thousand times easier to do the thing than stew about it. As Emerson so wisely put it, "Do the thing and you will have the power." Start today opening the way for constructive thinking and constructive action in your life. Take a long vacation from worry—and then make nonworry your habit pattern. You owe it to yourself. Keep knowing *God is there*.

EVERY PROBLEM KNOWN TO MAN HAS AN ANSWER

Often people think that their problems are special, their problems have no answers. This is not so. Every problem man can devise for himself has an answer, a perfect right solution. *Nothing is impossible to God working through you.*

Let's take some of the problems that are common today and see how they can be met. Here is a list of problems that come across my desk most often. Perhaps yours will be among them.

Q. I have an incurable disease, the doctors have no answer for this one. I'm doomed.

A. There are no incurable diseases. If God's perfect Life

is everywhere present, the Presence envelops every man, woman, and child. In Truth, the real *you* has never been ill, never sinned, never suffered. Once the false concept is healed there will be a corresponding change in the body. I have seen all manner of sickness healed. Know that God is able. Work to fill your mind with a spiritual awareness and your body will glorify God.

Q. I worry that there won't be enough money to go around. It's all very well for you to say that there can be prosperity for someone in business, but I am on a pension. Where am I going to get any more?

A. I wish you could see the letters I get from pensioners. Once these people turned to the true Source for their supply they were amazed to find that they received from unexpected avenues; the money they had seemed to go farther and was extended by free rides, and gifts of various sorts. There are so many answers once we open our minds to receive them. God has ways we know not of, but we will never discover them as long as our minds are occupied with thoughts of worry. Lift your consciousness to thoughts of Abundance and your circumstances will constantly improve.

Q. I have trouble making a decision. I'm afraid to act because I might make a mistake. What if I make the wrong decision?

A. The person who fears making a decision spends endless hours of futile travel down imaginary roads all leading to defeat. Perhaps you cannot trust yourself to make the right decision, but you can trust the infinite Intelligence right within you to see around the corners. Know that you will be divinely guided and then trust that Guidance when it comes. *Trust in the Lord with all thine heart; and lean not unto thine own understanding. In all thy ways acknowledge Him and He shall direct thy paths.*[1]

1 Proverbs 3: 5, 6.

Q. I am a student. When faced with an examination I panic. My mind becomes a blank. How can I stop worrying about tests?

A. Students have a wonderful opportunity to prove that *God is there,* working in and through them. You will remember that Jesus said, *Of myself I can do nothing; the Father within doeth the works.* Know that of yourself you may not have the answers, but God is never at a loss. All that has ever been known, all that will ever be known is already known to the divine Mind. Mind is All-Knowing. You can paraphrase the words of Jesus: "Of myself I can do nothing; the Wisdom within me doeth the works." Start trusting the Wisdom within you and you will be amazed how your life will open up. Ideas will come to you that you had not thought of. Ideas will come out of the blue. Trust in the Power that is All-Power and you will never be disappointed. It works for the student, the businessman, the author, the musician, the actor, the housewife. It makes no difference. Open yourself to receive the divine Power and you need never again worry.

SELF-DIRECTION

I am not afraid.
I am living in the present.
I trust the future to be supplied with all that I need.
I will meet each day as it comes, knowing God is there.

XVI WHY LET FEAR CONQUER YOU—YOU CONQUER IT!

> *The direst foe of courage is the fear itself, not the object of it; and the man who can overcome his own terror is a hero and more.*
>
> GEORGE MACDONALD

FEAR is the number one enemy of mankind. At least once in every generation some great man comes along to remind us *there is nothing to fear but fear itself.* Whenever a strong man leads his people out of the valley of fear he is greatly revered.

Such a man was Sir Winston Churchill. His passing reminded us again of his great leadership during World War II. When he raised his fingers in the famous V-for-Victory symbol, each one who saw him was inspired with some of his strength and courage, his undefeatable will to win. It is true that fear is contagious, but so is courage contagious. Churchill elected to live by courage and his influence is felt even today. When death and destruction threatened his beloved London, he stood firm. Because of his faith, the people of Britain stood firm with him. There must have been times when he secretly doubted. Through courage and love of country he overcame those doubts.

WHERE DOES FEAR COME FROM?

For God hath not given us the spirit of fear; but of power, and of love, and of a sound mind,[1] the Bible tells us. Where,

[1] II Timothy 1:7.

then, does fear come from? There is no basic fear common to all men; all of man's fears are acquired. Every fear that man has acquired can be dissolved through an understanding of God—through the power and the love and the sound mind within him.

Suppose you step up to a person and say, "Is there anything that you are afraid of?" He will probably answer, "Of course not!" We don't like to admit our fears because when we do we are pointing up our weaknesses. But, on thinking it over the person may admit, "Well, I might be afraid of freeways—traffic nowadays is rough, and I might be afraid of going down a dark street late at night—I read, just the other day, that someone was hit over the head . . ." After awhile he might think of many fears that he hadn't really acknowledged consciously to himself. Down, down into his subconscious mind he had pressed them, covering them over with a surface of false bravado; but underneath, his fears had linked themselves together in a chain of fear that had become unreasonable anxiety, a sort of general uneasiness that he attributed to the times until he could not really put his finger on any one thing that was the important fear in his life.

FREEDOM DOES NOT DEPEND UPON OUTER CONDITIONS

The greatest man who ever lived, the man who lived the Christ as an example for us all, directed much of his teaching toward the overcoming of fear.

Let not your heart be troubled, neither let it be afraid,[2] *Fear not, little flock; for it is your Father's good pleasure to give you the kingdom.*[3]

Jesus knew what courage was. The country in which he

2 John 14:27.
8 Luke 12:32.

lived was overrun by conquerors. Roman soldiers were everywhere demanding that the conquered people maintain them and feed them. Jesus taught that individual freedom must be found within, freedom that does not depend upon outer conditions. The kingdom he spoke of is inner dominion through an understanding of the Power and Intelligence that overcomes all doubt and sets man free.

COURAGE WILL WIN—COURAGE IS OF GOD

Today, as in the time of Jesus, people are tempted to fear the future. This time it is not the Romans but the communists who seem to be making great inroads that challenge our freedom. Fear is not the answer. Again the answer is courage. Stand firm. Your courage will be contagious; it will spread and influence others. Your faith will sustain all who know you. Courage will win because courage is of God. "Truth crushed to earth will rise again." God is omnipotent. Know that infinite Intelligence works through you. There is no power in error no matter how we name the enemy. God is the only Power and God Power lives through you.

HOW TO DEAL WITH FEAR

Remember this, you cannot reason with fear. Fear is an emotion. It is not reasonable or rational. There is always an object of fear and about this object we build up a feeling which is not the Truth. Fear becomes exaggerated. You cannot reason with your fears, but you can bring them out into the open and see them for what they are—nothing trying to be something. You can start, then, with Truth, and reason from there. There is an answer concealed within every problem. There is an answer to every fear, that answer is to be found in the Truth about the problem. To find it we must be willing to face the fear and prove its nothingness.

HOW ONE MAN FACED HIS FEAR AND OVERCAME IT

Down in the South where I came from there are many rivers, deep and wide. At the bends of certain of these rivers there are whirlpools which are considered to be extremely dangerous to anyone who is caught in them. It has been said that very few people come out of them alive.

One day a young man stood on the bank of a river observing a whirlpool. He watched a log being swallowed up by the whirling water only to reappear downstream a few seconds later. He asked himself, "Why does anyone need to be afraid of a whirlpool?" After some thoughtful moments he undressed and dived into the river. Refusing to be frightened, he allowed himself to be carried into the swirling water. Around and around he went. Then, holding his breath, and with arms held at his side, he was sucked down. Moments later he bobbed safely to the surface beyond the turbulence, just as the log had. Swimming to shore, he felt victorious. He smiled to himself. Never again need he fear the whirlpools. He thought to himself, "Once you know the Truth about a thing there is nothing to fear."

Not only had his experience with the whirlpool taught him not to fear whirlpools, but it had taught him how to meet life. He had been willing to take a calculated risk in order to prove that life is orderly, that life is governed by law. He had drawn upon Wisdom and Love in order to have the confidence to go into the whirlpool and emerge safely. He had had to trust every step of the way. Had he panicked at any time he might have caused great harm to himself. Panic is fear run rampant and always more harm comes from the fear than from the thing feared.

LOVE CASTS OUT FEAR

Here is another story that illustrates the role that fear plays in our lives. A man had a Doberman Pinscher dog, a little pup three months old, of which he was very fond. Because of business reasons, it was necessary for him to move to another city, and so he gave his dog to a friend. About a year later he had occasion to return to his hometown and, of course, the first thing he wanted to do was see his dog. He was surprised to see that his friend had erected a high fence around the house and that at the gate there was a bell. He knew that the bell was to attract the owner of the house, but seeing the dog on the porch he called to it. The dog paid no attention to him, but he decided to go in and have a few words with the dog. When he entered the gate the dog's hackles went up and he growled. As the man, without fear, continued to approach, the dog began to quiet down. By the time the man reached the porch he was wagging his tail—the dog, I mean! They played together for a few minutes before the man went to the door and knocked. His friend opened the door and greeted him warmly. They visited for a few moments, and then, all of a sudden the man of the house turned pale—"The dog," he said. "Did you walk right through the yard and past the dog?" "Why, yes, of course," said his visitor. "Prince and I are old friends. At first he did not recognize me, but that was not for long."

"That is not Prince," was the reply. "Prince died shortly after you left and we got another dog like him, but this one is a killer. That is the reason for the high fence."

Because there was no fear, there was no danger. Love had bridged the gap. Upon leaving, the man refused his friend's offer to escort him to the gate. As he passed the dog, the dog looked at him and growled slightly. Fear crept into the man's thought. He began to reason, "This dog is not my dog. He is a killer." Walking faster and faster, he got to the gate just in time. The love for the dog was contagious when he first went into the yard. Even though the dog was considered to be a killer, he responded with friendliness. As the man left the yard, fear and doubt crept in and were also felt by the dog, causing the dog to respond in fear.

All too often we let ourselves be governed by circumstances. When the man heard that the dog had the reputation of being a killer he lost his confidence. Had he known and trusted the Truth of his being, he could have proved that perfect love casts out fear and makes us one with all of life. Fear has deceptive ways. We are always deceived by the thing that we fear. In this case, it was the *reputation* of the dog, another time it might be the *threat* of Communism or the *shadow* of death.

FEAR IS THE STRONGEST WEAPON THE ENEMY HAS

It doesn't matter who or what you consider to be your enemy, his strongest weapon is your fear. The moment you start to fear this enemy, it has taken power over you. An ancient legend illustrates this. It goes like this:

I met Death. I inquired, "Where are you going?"

Death replied, "I am on my way to Benares."

"Why are you going there?" I asked.

"To kill a thousand men."

The next week I met Death again.

I asked Death, "You went to Benares to kill a thousand men? I understand that one hundred thousand are dead."

Death smiled and said, "I killed one thousand. Fear killed the rest."

Let's take a look at some of these fears. As we look at them we will begin to look through them. Once we have seen through them we can have no fear about them.

OVERCOMING THE FEAR OF DEATH

It has been said, "Cowards die many times." Every fear is a little death. Basically every fear is a fear of death. It is only when we cease to fear death that we are able to face life fearlessly. Death has been called "the last enemy"; actually it is the first enemy that we should overcome if we are to enjoy abundant living.

Is death really an enemy? Is it not rather our feeling about death that should be destroyed? Death comes only to the body. It does not touch the Spirit. It is our belief about death that needs to be changed that it may cease to be an enemy. Nothing can happen to Life. Life cannot die. Once a person understands this, death can have no power over him. Life is eternal. The form that it uses may change but Life goes on forever. Life is indestructible.

The mind of man is one with the Universal Mind. The real Self of you can never die. It will continue on in an ever unfolding, continuous experience, drawing to itself whatever it needs to express. Death is only a momentary pause in our forward motion so that we may move into another experience. As Sir Thomas Browne so beautifully put it, "The created world is but a small parenthesis in eternity."

Once having overcome the fear of death it is easy to overcome the fear of disease. Dis-ease is simply lack of ease; discomfort, perhaps, but not a power. There is no power in disease. When we let ourselves entertain anxieties, worries, and the other children of fear, we sometimes leave ourselves open to a sense of separation from Life resulting in a belief of disease in the body. Since this is not the Truth about us, it can be overcome. God did not establish disease in our bodies. God gave us perfect Life. It is for us to accept it without fear.

LACK HAS NO POWER OF ITS OWN

How can we fear lack when we realize that there is an infinite Source from which we draw in this experience. Man's greed, man's fear of the future is simply insecurity. To overcome this fear, know that your security is of God, an inner condition that does not depend upon outer circumstances.

Lack is not a condition but an attitude of mind. Everything in life tends toward extravagant abundance. Man, through fear, is always trying to curtail this abundance.

The other day I cut open a grapefruit that, by count, contained sixty-five seeds. It must have been a throwback to the old days before seedless grapefruit. Nature intended every part of creation to be lavishly provided with the seed of future abundance. Today we are restricting everything, even seeds in grapefruit! Men are paid not to plant, not to work, and are often discouraged from having ideas. All these things represent attitudes that limit Life. Trust in Life's abundance and you will find that you need never fear lack. Think abundance! Dwell on the lavishness of Life. Think how many leaves there are on the trees, the number of grains of sand on the beach, the endless varieties of flowers and plants. There is plenty for all. Abundance is an attribute of Life and is therefore unlimited. Through Self-Direction this can be your experience.

HOW TO MASTER FEAR

We have seen that fear is giving power to the enemy. We draw to ourselves the very thing that we fear. In many instances we create an enemy out of whole cloth. The first step in overcoming fear is a better understanding of the object of the fear. If your fear concerns another person, have a talk with that person and try to understand what motivates him. Perhaps he acts the way he does because he fears what you may

do to him. Many times our fears are based purely on preju-
dice.

Examine your fears with an open mind—are they merely
old prejudices in new clothing? How many times we fear a
person because he reminds us of an old enemy! How often we
fear to go to a certain place where we have suffered in the
past!

God did not give us the spirit of fear but of Power, and of
Love, and of a sound mind. Is there some person you fear?
If God be for us who can be against us? [4] Think it over; why
are you afraid of that person? Your protection lies within you.
Establish a feeling of love instead. *Where the Spirit of the
Lord is, there is liberty.* Where Love is present there is freedom. *Perfect love casteth out fear.* Fear of man is simply lack
of trust in God within. Infinite Intelligence knows how to
meet the situations in life as they arise. There is no power in
personality. Trust in the Perfect Power and you will always
receive fair treatment. If Love is everywhere present, whom
can we fear?

SELF-DIRECTION

*There is nothing to fear. I live in a mental world in which I
have been given dominion. Right within me is the Power which
is able to meet any situation I shall ever encounter. All that I
need is within me right now.*

[4] Romans 8:31.

XVII   YES, YOU CAN STOP
SMOKING!

*The revelation of thought takes men out
of servitude into freedom.*

EMERSON

SPRING is the time when nature puts on a new dress, when
everything comes to us fresh and clean and beautiful. Spring
is a wonderful time of new beginnings. We begin to be tired
of our winter clothes and our winter thoughts. We plant new
seeds in the ground and we plant new seed thoughts in our
minds. We need not wait until spring, however, to take stock
and see if there is some area in our lives where we would like
to make a fresh start.

We are all pretty much creatures of habit. Do we really
want some of the habits we cling to, or have we let them become fixed because it is the path of least resistance?

WE CHOOSE OUR HABITS

An action so often repeated that it becomes a fixed charac-
teristic, or tendency, is considered to be a habit. A habit is not
necessarily a bad habit unless it deprives a person of his freedom to act creatively. We might say that any act which has
become a part of the subjective mentality is a habit. Habits
are formed by first consciously thinking and then uncon-
sciously acting. What one thinks today as a conscious thought
may, tomorrow, be a submerged *but active thought habit.*

From what we know about the working of the subconscious mind, it is clearly seen that the subconscious mind loves a habit. Being the seat of the memory, the ever faithful servant, is willing to carry out the orders given to it, no matter how repetitious these orders have become. You can see that a well-grooved habit is a veritable delight to the subconscious mind. "Goody, goody," says the subconscious mind, "here is a nice orderly habit. This is what I understand. This I can go to work on again and again until at last it becomes automatic action." It is sort of like putting a satellite into orbit. Once the subconscious mind has grooved a habit, the habit goes on and on *unless we consciously take command of the situation and do something about it*. Thank goodness, the conscious mind still has the last word or we would all be in bondage to our habits, good or bad.

> *Sow a thought and you reap an action.*
> *Sow an action and you reap a habit.*
> *Sow a habit and you reap a character.*
> *Sow a character and you reap a destiny.*

There are constructive habits and destructive habits. The subconscious mind is not a bit particular. It never judges. Since it operates entirely through the process of deductive reasoning, it happily goes to work on the order given. It will carry out our orders to the letter. We give the orders and the subconscious mind goes to work to honor our commands.

The other day a man called me on the telephone and accused me of saying something in a lecture that was responsible for causing him to be able to stop smoking. At first, he said, he wasn't sure that he was too happy about it.

"You just took a big spoon and stirred my life up," was the way he put it. "It was that bit about taking mental inventory once a year. I did what you said, taking stock of my habits and asking myself if they were really what I wanted carried out in my experience. I asked myself if they were beneficial to me physically, mentally, and spiritually. I even went a step further and asked myself if they were sometimes annoying to others. I asked myself if my mental habits were sowing seeds of destruction for me; if I habitually thought pessimistic thoughts, doubting myself, doubting others, doubting the future. And then, as you said, I asked myself if I really wanted to continue these habits that I had been nurturing so carefully. This was the point when I felt as if my life had been stirred up with a big spoon! It was like moving day. Everything was out in the middle of the room and it had to be put back in some sort of order before I could live in my mental house. It seemed up to me to put it back in good order and so I plunged right in.

"First, I took mental inventory of my day, and this was rough. It was apparent that I wasn't getting any smarter with the years. My day went something like this:

"I have a habit of starting each day by going to the door in my pajamas and dragging in the newspaper to see what dire calamity is reported on the front page—'Is that really the way I want to start my day?' I asked myself. Next, even before brushing my teeth, I light a cigarette, drawing the smoke deep into my lungs until my head swims. They say it is really bad for you and I feel sort of guilty about it. 'Do I really want to continue this habit?' I wondered. Next, I drink about ten cups of coffee during the morning. I feel a little uneasy about this, too, but it is such a habit. I reach for the cup by my elbow as I reach for that cigarette. They seem to go together. I've been doing it for years. 'Why do I do it?' I queried. I have the habit of skipping lunch. There's so much to do that I work right through the noon hour. It's just a habit, I guess. Along about four I start thinking of a cocktail. I make myself wait until five and then I hunt up the nearest bar. I really need a lift. I tell myself that it is just a habit. I can break it anytime I want, but I keep right on doing it.

"It wasn't a pretty picture. I began to ask myself, did I

really want to continue some of these habits? If man had been given dominion of his life and his thoughts, what was I doing letting a bunch of habits control each day? If my body is the *temple of the living God,* did I really want to treat it that way? Frankly, I'd been reading so many articles lately about the danger of smoking, I had become a little uneasy in spite of myself. I wondered if the doctors themselves were warning their own children not to smoke; if, as the papers and magazines say, seventy percent agree that it contributes to cancer, emphysema, and diseases of the heart and blood vessels; if the president of the State Board of Medical Examiners put out the word that there was no question that tobacco companies were selling a form of poison to the American people, a chemical, a dope; was it really intelligent to keep on smoking?

"I guess this all sounds pretty negative to you. Surely, it is information on the physical level. I know that you teach mind control. Granted, I might smoke and protect myself, in a measure, from the harmful effects; but who wants to spend all of his time undoing such harmful effects through mind concentration? I figured that no matter how faithful a person might be in declaring that tobacco had no power over him, a few of these statistics might sink in and the damage would be done. There would always be some little sneaky thought to overcome. Every time I read another story about lung cancer or cancer of the throat or mouth, I might be apt to associate it with myself. Every time I noticed a little extra hoarseness in my throat, shortness of breath, coughing, or heart palpitation, I would be apt to worry whether smoking was harming me. Right here, I asked myself if it was worth it to continue smoking. Honestly, Dr. Addington, isn't it sort of like standing in the middle of the freeway and praying to be protected from the oncoming traffic?"

"Well," I answered, "when Satan tempted Jesus to jump off the top of the temple to prove that he was protected by God, Jesus said: *It is written again, Thou shalt not tempt the*

Lord thy God. I think that if I felt that it was tempting the Law to smoke, I'd choose to stop."

"That's just what I did," he replied, "and frankly, I wonder why I ever did want to smoke in the first place. It was all because you said in your lecture, 'Yes, you can stop smoking, or any other habit that you would like to change. It is easy when you understand the law of Self-Direction.' The trouble is that once I found that I didn't have to smoke, I decided that I'd change a lot of other habits that weren't doing me any good and that's why my life seems to be stirred up right now."

YES, YOU CAN STOP SMOKING

Yes, you can stop smoking, or overcome any other habit. It is all a matter of the direction you give the subconscious mind. Let's take smoking. Many people say to me, wistfully, "I'd like to stop smoking, but I can't." When this happens, I know that they really don't want to stop smoking. Once one desires to be free of smoking, everything necessary to bring this desire about will be done. The question is: do you really want to stop smoking? If you really want to stop, I will tell you how. This is the way, walk ye in it:

1. Do you choose to stop smoking? It must be your choice.
2. Always give the orders to your subconscious mind in the affirmative. The subconscious mind does not understand a negative order. If you say, "I am not going to smoke any more," the attention is still on smoking. The order should be: "I am free from the smoking habit."
3. Set up a new chain reaction, a new sequence of motor response for yourself.
4. Accept yourself as already free from the smoking habit.

The first step is to choose to stop smoking. Do you really desire to stop smoking? Maybe you just want to prove to yourself that you *can't* stop smoking. If you choose to stop smoking and believe that you *can,* giving positive orders to your sub-conscious mind, you will definitely cease from the smoking habit. *That is all it is, just a habit pattern.*

You must make the choice and believe that it is already accomplished. *What things soever ye desire when ye pray, be-lieve that ye receive them, and ye shall have them.* This is the Truth about overcoming the smoking habit. If you set up a new, constructive order for your subconscious mind, it will immediately go to work to prove that order instead of the old one. *Yes, you can stop smoking!* Do you really want to stop smoking?

Too often, people fail because they find themselves trying to do something that they really do not want to do. They have to prove that they *can't* stop smoking. They are giving lip service to the idea of stopping, but underneath they are rebelling at the idea. Perhaps they say that they are trying to stop to please mother, husband, or wife, or maybe their own guilty conscience, but down deep they have no intention of stopping. When a person says to me, "I'd like to stop smoking, but . . . ," this is generally the case. If you continue to smoke, it is because you actually choose to do so. The habit of smok-ing really has no power over you but the power you give it.

DOES PRACTICE MAKE PERFECT?

Practice makes perfect is an old adage that has been re-peated so often that people have come to believe it. *Practice makes perfect* only if the habit pattern is perfect to begin with. The subconscious mind is precise and careful. It loves to groove an act. Every golfer knows that if he practices a poor golf swing long enough he has a poor golf swing grooved. That is why golfers take lessons so that they can start all over and get the right swing grooved. *Practice does not always make perfect, but practice makes automatic.* To be a great pianist, you have to practice the piano correctly. Only then will the practice prove beneficial.

If you practice a habit it will become engraved in your mind, even though that habit is something you do not want to experience. Through Self-Direction, *you can change any habit*. The conscious mind is still king. You still can take dominion. The habit may seem to have taken complete control, but the conscious mind can turn the tide. It is true that unless we control our thought, it will control us. *Through Self-Direction we can control our thought and thus our habit patterns*.

THE SUBCONSCIOUS MIND RESPONDS TO POSITIVE INSTRUCTION

The subconscious mind will always respond to positive direction. It does not understand the reverse approach. If you say that you will not do something, you will end up doing the very thing that you do not want to do. The subconscious mind just does not understand a negative order. If you say to yourself, "I will not forget to close the door when I go out," you can bet your bottom dollar that you will go out and leave the door open, but, if you say, instead, "When I go out I will remember to close the door," you have given the subconscious mind a constructive order.

This constructive approach must be followed through in every area. If we say, "I'll never be able to get up in time in the morning,"—so it will be. You will sleep right through the clock's alarm if necessary, to prove that the law you have set up will be carried out to the letter. The ever willing subconscious mind believes that it is serving you with precision. However, if you say, "I will awaken at exactly six o'clock in the morning," it will wake you on the dot. There is a clock inside you that is always accurate. The electric clock may stop during the night due to power failure, but the clock inside of you will wake you exactly at six o'clock. If you do not believe me, try it.

SET UP A NEW CHAIN REACTION

Smoking is an oral satisfaction. It does not nourish the body or improve the mind. We smoke to be good to ourselves. A person draws on a cigarette the way a baby draws on a pacifier. It is a nursing action; a desire to express life; to receive love; to be nourished by life just as a baby instinctively starts moving its mouth in an effort to nurse. Sometimes, simply understanding this takes away all desire to smoke. However, if a person has become more or less in bondage to chain reaction, he needs to break this pattern. Start out by setting up a new response to the idea of smoking. Think of yourself as taking a firm stand when someone offers you a cigarette. Hear yourself saying, calmly but firmly, "No, I don't smoke." Get this firmly grooved in your mind until there is no decision to be made. You have already made this decision.

Now, we can deal with the motor response. When the urge comes to go through the little ritual of lighting up a cigarette —taking out the pack, shaking out the cigarette, tapping the tobacco down, lighting up, the first drag etc., etc.—set up a new sequence for yourself. Many have met this step by carrying around a package of mints, preferably the kind that are individually wrapped. Take one out, unwrap it slowly and methodically, and pop it into your mouth. Don't worry about gaining weight, you'll soon feel so much peppier that the weight will adjust itself. Another little ritual that I recommend is to carefully take out your pen or pencil and a little card that you have provided for the purpose and write down: "I do not choose to smoke," or "I no longer smoke; I am free from the smoking habit." See how many little cards it takes before this new order has become so thoroughly grooved in your subconscious mind that the very thought of smoking will seem foreign to you. When this takes place you will no longer need the cards because you will have become free.

A MATTER OF TAKING CONTROL

Remember, these instructions are only for those who desire to stop smoking. I believe that with spiritual growth comes unfoldment at every level, inspiration at the spiritual level, guidance in right thinking, and right living at the physical level. Those who are on the spiritual path find that sooner or later smoking *leaves them*. If you really choose to be free of this habit, or any other habit for that matter, you can be completely free in one to three days with never a backward look.

SELF-DIRECTION

I choose to stop smoking. I choose to be free. I am a non-smoker. When someone offers me a cigarette, I say with authority, "No, thank you, I do not smoke." Whenever I am tempted to smoke and pick up a cigarette, I tear it into little pieces and throw it in the wastebasket. I am free.

XVIII INSOMNIA IS NOT
FOR YOU

Insomnia is a phantom peril.
JOSEPHINE A. JACKSON, M.D.

Do you toss and turn at night, waiting in vain for sleep to come and knit up that raveled sleeve of care? Or are you, like myself, one of the fortunate ones who fall asleep as soon as the head touches the pillow?

Judging by the number of sleeping pills purchased each year in the United States alone, the former group must far exceed the latter. Let's examine a few of the things that seem to come between people and sleep.

THAT PHANTOM PERIL—INSOMNIA

"To sleep or not to sleep! That is the question. In all the world there is nothing to equal it in importance,—to the man with insomnia. His days are mere interludes between troubled nights spent in restless tossing to and fro and feverish worry over the weary day to come. His mind, filled with ideas about the disastrous effects of insomnia, he imagines himself fast sliding down hill toward the grave or the insane-asylum," writes Dr. Josephine Jackson.[1]

[1] Josephine A. Jackson, M.D., *Outwitting Our Nerves*, (New York: The Century Co., 1921).

During her years of practice, Dr. Jackson treated many people who were *suffering,* and I use the term advisedly, with insomnia. She discovered that the fear of insomnia was based upon ignorance of the difference between enforced wakefulness and deliberate wakefulness—insomnia. Insomnia, Dr. Jackson discovered, was a habit. One who had acquired this habit, she found, could stay awake almost indefinitely without harm.

In her book, *Outwitting Our Nerves,* she cites case after case of people who had gone through life sleeping little, if at all. She proves by her illustrations that people can live long lives with insomnia because insomnia is nothing more or less than a habit, and *habit spells ease.* She says that since the brain cells are not irritated during insomnia, because there is no effort to keep awake, virtually no energy is expended—except in restless tossing and worry. "If the body is kept still and emotion eliminated, fatigue products are washed away and the reserves are filled in with perfect ease."

Dr. Jackson calls insomnia "thinking in circles." She goes on to say:

Habit means automatic, subconscious activity, with the least expenditure of energy and the least amount of fatigue. We have already noted the ease with which heart and diaphragm muscles carry on their work from the beginning of life to its end. Anything relegated to the subconscious mind can be kept up almost indefinitely without tire, and to this subconscious type of activity belong the thoughts of a chronic insomniac. Despite all assertions to the contrary, his conscious mind is not really awake. If he is questioned about the happenings of the night, he is likely to have been unaware of the most audible noises. The thoughts that run through his brain are not new, constructive, energy-consuming thoughts, but the same old thoughts that have been going around in circles for days and weeks at a time.

Dr. Jackson compares these thoughts to a horse that knows the rounds and goes jogging on indefinitely without guidance from the driver.

The thing that tires one out, Dr. Jackson points out, is not the insomnia but the emotion over the insomnia; that people who are perpetually fagged out, are not suffering from the loss of sleep, but from the worry; the tossing and turning; the endless exclaiming, "Why don't I sleep? How badly I will feel tomorrow! What a night! What a night!"

MYTHS ABOUT SLEEP

Dr. Julius Segal, who has become quite an authority on sleep, lists in his book *Insomnia* [2] some of the interesting myths about sleep.

> In their studies of sleep, scientists have encountered the many myths about insomnia that have accumulated through the years—a secret mythology of sleep passed on by friends and relatives, most of which deserves a thorough debunking.
>
> Many really believe, for example, that there is an "eight-hour law," a dictate from heaven, saying that homo sapiens must spend eight hours each night in delightful oblivion.
>
> People blame nights of poor sleep upon changes in weather, the presence of a cat in the house, strange phenomena seen and unseen, a closet door left open, or just an uncomfortable state or malaise.

He believes that one of the most dangerous sleep myths of our day is that a person can simply swallow a pill to cure insomnia. He calls this a dangerous course of chemical warfare. A survey of the drug industry indicates the magnitude of this rush to the medicine cabinet. In one year alone Americans spent about $300 million on tranquilizers.

[2] Gay G. Luce and Julius Segal, *Insomnia: The Guide for Troubled Sleepers*, (New York: Doubleday, 1969).

IS THE POWER IN THE DRUG OR THE BELIEF
ABOUT THE DRUG?

I am reminded of the story of a friend of mine who had reached the point where she felt that she could no longer go on without a good night's sleep. One evening she was visiting a friend and, as usual, the conversation got around to her problem, that terrible bug-a-boo, insomnia.

"I simply can't face one more night of tossing and turning, trying to sleep!" she remarked as she buttoned her coat to drive home.

With loving concern, her friend left the room and came back with a large capsule and a glass of water. "I have just the thing for you," she said, "but you must go right home, don't stop along the way or you will fall asleep at the wheel."

Ah, blessed relief in sight. The visitor downed the pill and with a grateful sigh prepared to go right home and claim that good night's sleep. When she got home she was almost too sleepy to get undressed. She tumbled into bed and slept the sleep of the just, ten hours or more.

Thrilled over the capsule that had brought such restful sleep, she called her benefactor the next morning to find out where she could get more of this wonder medicine.

Her friend burst out laughing. "Did it really make you sleep?"

"Why, yes, what's so funny?"

"The capsule I gave you was nothing but vitamin B one," her friend replied.

My friend got the point and laughed with her. It was obvious that the power lay *in the belief about the capsule rather than in the capsule itself*. Perhaps this accounts for the fact that many times sleeping potions fail to bring sleep after habitual use of the drug.

A NOVEL CURE FOR INSOMNIA

A lieutenant on a destroyer during World War II told me this story. He had been waking up at about two-thirty every morning, unable to go back to sleep. Fortunately, there was on board, temporarily, a doctor. The young officer decided to take his problem to the doctor, thinking that the doctor would provide him with some sleeping pills. The doctor heard him out. "These are orders," he said. "When you awaken in the morning at two-thirty, get fully dressed, go to the galley and get yourself a cup of coffee, and then go to the bridge and report for duty. Stay on duty for the rest of the night. Continue with your regular day duties."

This startled the lieutenant. However, the doctor out-ranked him, and there was nothing he could do but accept the orders. The next morning at two-thirty when he awoke he got dressed and did as he had been told. The following day he checked in with the doctor and was given the same orders. The next morning when he awakened at two-thirty, he quickly closed his eyes and went right back to sleep. That was the end of his insomnia!

HOW TO GO TO SLEEP

Dr. Jackson found that the best way to learn to sleep is not to care whether you do or not. The best way to do this is to erase once and for all that old rule about having to have so many hours sleep per night. She proved to her patients that they could rest almost as well without sleep as with it, *providing they kept the mind calm and the body relaxed.*

It has been said, "Don't look for sleep; it flies away like a pigeon when one pursues it."

It has been found that attention to anything keeps the mind awake, and this applies most of all to sleep. Insomniacs often wake themselves up to see if they are sleeping! But this is not just a matter of fooling ourselves. Once we become convinced that sleep is not absolutely necessary, that our bodies will take what rest they need, we will have overcome the very anxiety that has kept us from sleeping. Insomnia will then have no importance and it will soon disappear.

ARE YOU SURE YOU DON'T PREFER THE LATE-LATE SHOW?

A relative of mine whom everyone in the family adored was plagued by insomnia. She claimed that she slept only one or, at the most, two hours a night. Since she lived to a ripe age and passed away asleep in her chair one night after dinner, she was living proof that insomnia is not as dangerous as people think it is. This aunt, we always felt, secretly preferred her nocturnal projects to sleep. She enjoyed the late-late show on television and endless "who-done-its." She drank a fantastic amount of coffee during the day, as well as during the night and got up often to smoke. While we commiserated with her dutifully when she spoke of her difficulty, we all privately believed that she arranged her nights by choice.

A FEW RULES FOR THOSE WHO WOULD ENJOY SOUND, RELAXED SLEEP

Have you been having trouble sleeping? Here are a few rules that will give you sound, relaxed sleep. I guarantee that they will work if you will follow them, that is, if you are honestly tired of your insomnia and don't just want to prove to me that nothing on earth can keep you from lying awake!

1. Go to bed to sleep. Expect to sleep. Let your every act in preparation for bed suggest sleep. Avoid stimulating reading, detective stories, or political discussions that get your adrenaline up. Bedtime is not the time to fight. Resolutely put out of your mind any thought about tomorrow's big project.

As the great Teacher said, *Take therefore no thought for the morrow; for the morrow shall take thought for the things of itself.* Rather, meditate upon something that gives you a sense of release, such as the twenty-third Psalm. I often use this little poem by Henry Van Dyke.

DROP THY BURDEN AND THY CARE

> Ere thou sleepest, gently lay
> Every troubled thought away.
> Put off worry and distress
> As thou putest off thy dress
> Drop thy burden and thy care
> In the quiet arms of prayer.
> Lord, Thou knowest how I live,
> All I've done amiss, forgive.
> All the good I've tried to do,
> Strengthen, bless and carry through.
> All I love in safety keep,
> While in Thee I fall asleep.

2. Before going to sleep rule out all thought of past mistakes and failures. No one can sleep if he mulls over the mistakes and hurts of the day in bed. If you are tempted to do this, try reconciling the day that is over. Go back through the day and forgive everyone whom you think has hurt you. Now, forgive yourself for every mistake you think you have made, irrespective of how stupid you thought yourself. Did you speak out sharply to someone and then blame yourself afterward? How do you know that your remark was not the very thing needed to set him to thinking? Whatever the day held, release it. You did the best that you could at the moment. Now it is over and done with. Tomorrow will be another day. *Drop thy burden and thy care.* Life holds nothing against you. Let it go. Surrender your life and affairs to the Power within you that knows how to make everything right.

3. Under no circumstances worry about not sleeping. The hours spent lying quietly in bed will do you just as much good as sleeping.

Suppose you are one of those three o'clock planners. Subjectively you choose to wake up and do your planning at night. Actually, it seems to be the only time of the day when you can be alone with your own thoughts. Keep a pad and pencil by your bedside to jot down your ideas and plans and you will find that you then can release them and go back to sleep easily. Losing this hour of sleep will not be damaging to you. Your body will make it up during the next sleep cycle.

4. Try counting your blessings instead of sheep. Sleep comes with a feeling of contentment. Worry, anxiety, no matter how carefully we conceal it from ourselves, will tend to keep us awake. Instead of struggling with what you don't have, try making a mental list of the good things in your life. No matter how gloomy the picture, there is always something for which to be thankful. Things are never as dire as they seem. Give it a try. You'll be surprised how many things you have on the plus side. Soon you will find a warm feeling of contentment stealing over you as you fall asleep.

5. Look up the quotations on sleep in the Bible. They are sleep producers in themselves.

> *I laid me down and slept: I awakened, for the Lord sustained me.* Psalms 3:5

There is a whole sermon in this one. We can lay this body down and sleep in perfect confidence knowing that the great Involuntary Life is sustaining us. Even while we sleep it keeps our hearts beating, takes care of our digestive functions, circulates our blood and maintains all the rest of the marvelous work of the body. It builds new body cells, as we sleep, and sloughs off the old. All this wonderful care we take for granted. We never think of giving thanks for the wonder of the subconscious mind. Can we not also trust the Infinite to care for our larger body, the body of our affairs? As we sleep the work is being done for us. Many hands procure and prepare the food that we will eat tomorrow. Others edit and print the newspaper we take for granted at our breakfast table. There are so many things we take for granted. Just think, all the thought seeds we have planted in mind are growing as we sleep. Let go and let God take care of you. Trust in the Perfect Power within you and you will soon fall asleep.

RELAXED SLEEP COMES THROUGH SELF-DIRECTION

Through the self directive power of the mind you can give instructions to your mind that will result in the subconscious mind taking over the sleep function. The next time you find yourself lying awake, try talking to yourself something like this: "I am now going to sleep. My whole body is relaxed. My mind is still. I am at peace. I am now ready for sleep. I am going to sleep for —— number of hours. I will awaken at —— o'clock rested and refreshed."

SELF-DIRECTION

I have no fear of lying awake; I do not have to make sleep come.
I have no regrets for the past and no anxiety for the future.
I now release all contentious thoughts.
I forgive myself and everyone else for past mistakes.
My mind is relaxed; I am filled with peace.
I lie down in trust and let sleep come.

XIX ANTIDOTE
FOR DISCOURAGEMENT

Serene I fold my hands and wait,
Nor care for wind or tide or sea;
I rave no more 'gainst time or fate,
For lo! My own shall come to me.
JOHN BURROUGHS

Discouragement comes to all of us at one time or another. No one is immune to it, although it is not a necessary ingredient of life. Its causes are varied, for it is due entirely to reliance upon human judgment. Without human judgment, there can be no discouragement.

To contemplate the meaning of the word discourage is discouraging in itself. The word courage is from the French *cour + age,* meaning, "of the heart." Discourage means "to dishearten," "to lessen courage," "to deprive of confidence," "to become faint of heart." It is one of those negative words which we try to avoid, like failure, depression, dismal, dreary, gloomy, melancholy, and cheerless—it carries a feeling of discouragement. Actually, it is not the words that should be avoided, but the feeling that accompanies those words.

DISAPPOINTMENT AND HOW TO MEET IT

A distinction should be made between disappointment and discouragement. Disappointment, if properly met, need not turn into discouragement. When our hopes or expectations involving people and circumstances are not fulfilled, we say that we are disappointed. A disappointment is neutralized when a new hope or a new expectation is set up to take the place of the unfulfilled one.

Blessing each situation for good, brings forth the good in the situation. *All things work together for good to them that love good.*[1]

If our motives are honest, if our attention is directed to the perfect Power within, we can expect that any change in the direction our lives are taking is for good for all concerned.

Suppose a father is disappointed because his son decides not to go to college. Great plans and sacrifices have been made so that the boy should have the opportunity that the father himself did not have and now his hopes are dashed. The father need not become discouraged. He should look for the good in the situation and refrain from judgment and condemnation. He should realize that this decision on the part of his son took courage, was perhaps hard for him to make, and that each one must live his own life in the way that is right for him. The lack of a college education does not mean that a person is necessarily doomed to failure. Many become stronger by getting out and facing life, meeting the challenges of life, instead of living the cloistered life in a university or college. Perhaps the son will want this education at a later date and be willing to make a greater effort for himself at that time. At any rate, the hopes and expectations that one has for another must coincide with the hopes and desires of the other person. The father should know that divine Intelligence working in and through his son will guide and direct him in the path that is right for him. Each one is a unique individualization of Spirit and for each there is a perfect plan known and revealed to him at his own point of awareness in the One Mind.

A business man who has high hopes and expectations for a

[1] Romans 8:28.

certain venture which does not materialize, should immediately shift his attention to another venture. The Ford Motor Company lost $265 million on the Edsel. Who remembers that loss now? Dwelling upon failure will only produce more failure. Disappointment is a temporary thing. It is how one meets it that counts. It is when one lets failure or dashed expectations cause him to lose heart, when he gives in to discouragement, that he is in dangerous territory.

One who is tempted by discouragement must realize that he is not alone, that everyone suffers disappointment at some time or other. We cannot always judge, from the human standpoint, what is best for ourselves. Our human tendency is to set up hopes and expectations so very high that disappointment often results. Yet, high expectations cause us to stretch, thereby using inner resources we did not realize we had.

A MOMENTARY SLUMP MAY BE A BLESSING

Every now and then we go into a slump, a low period. These slump periods are natural. They should not be looked upon with alarm, but should be times when we are preparing for renewal, for the period of uprise and the time of greater accomplishment. Quiet study and meditation are necessary. These are the productive times. Actually, the real work is done in the Silence and often a day spent at home completely inactive will be the day wherein we are given just the inspiration that is needed. Often, it is the only time we are quiet enough to hear our Guidance.

Let's not confuse our slumps with discouragement. Man was not made to travel at a continuously high pitch. There is an ebb and flow to all of life. As the preacher says in Ecclesiates:

> *To every thing there is a season, and a time to every purpose under heaven:*

*A time to be born, and a time to die; a time to plant, and a
time to pluck up that which is planted.
He hath made everything beautiful in his time.*

Ecclesiastes 3:1, 2, 11.

IN QUIET CONFIDENCE WE FIND OUR STRENGTH

The strength that comes to us through quiet and meditation shows us that it is important that we slow down and take
time for periods of relaxation.

One of the earliest lessons given to man was that he should
take one day out of seven in which to rest and give attention
to the higher values in life. Not only is this day one for worshipping God but it is a day in which we show that we trust
God because we do not feel that we have to be giving our full
attention seven days a week to business or the acquisition of
things. The word Sabbath means "to rest from labor." It is
the time when we let go and let God.

*In returning and rest shall ye be saved; in quietness and in
confidence shall be your strength.*

Isaiah 30:15

EVEN JESUS FACED DISCOURAGEMENT

Everyone at some time or another passes through discouraging times. Even Jesus, who had true dominion through the
Christ within, had his time of discouragement. He had
worked with his disciples for three years and had taught them
the innermost secrets of life. These twelve men were able to
heal the sick and cast out demons and to do all manner of
good things. Yet, in the fourteenth chapter of St. Mark it is
told that Peter vehemently declared his loyalty to Jesus and
that he would die for him. The other disciples also insisted
that they would, too. Jesus knew that this was not so, and that

they would be looking after their own interests in the time of trial. He took Peter, James, and John with him to the Mount of Olives. There he asked them to wait for him while he went apart to pray. He fell on the ground and prayed that if it were possible, the hour might pass from him. He said, "Dear Father, all things are possible to you, please, let me not have to drink this cup. Yet it is not what I want but what you want." [2]

Then he came and found them fast asleep. He spoke to Peter, "Are you asleep, Simon? Couldn't you have managed to have watched a single hour? Watch and pray, all of you, that you may not have to face temptation. Your Spirit is willing, but human nature is weak." [3]

Then he went away again and prayed in the same words and once more he came and found them asleep. They could not keep their eyes open and they did not know what to say for themselves. When he came back for the third time, he said, "Are you still going to sleep and take your ease? All right . . . the moment has come; now you are going to see the son of man betrayed into the hands of evil men! Wake up, let us be going! Look, here comes my betrayer!" [4]

His betrayer was none other than one of his own disciples. During this period, he must have had a feeling of discouragement. Yes, there were times when Jesus was discouraged. The antidote that he used is the antidote that we can use: prayer.

Discouragement arises out of our feelings about people, circumstances, and conditions. It is the feeling of being hemmed in and frustrated. It is the feeling of futility that comes when our dreams and ambitions all seem to come to naught. Washington felt the pangs of discouragement at Valley Forge during that cold and bleak winter. He had no backing from his congress; the men were deserting like flies; the

2 J. B. Phillips, *The Gospels*, (New York: Macmillan Co., 1955).
3 Ibid.
4 Ibid

ones who stayed were underfed, cold, and miserable. He had to trust in Something that he could neither see nor touch. *We walk by faith, not by sight,* said Paul.

NOTHING IS AGAINST US

Yesterday a man was in my office telling me how he had overcome discouragement. He told me that a year ago things looked dark, indeed. It seemed as though the people in his life had taken advantage of him in every way. Judging by appearance, he had every right to be discouraged. *Judge not according to the appearance, but judge righteous judgment,* admonished Jesus. This man steadfastly followed this advice.

According to appearances, he had no money at all, but he told me that he held to the truth that even the seeming lack of money was not against him. He worked on the premise *Nothing is against me—not even the lack of money is against me.* He told himself over and over until he thoroughly believed it, "God is all there is, everywhere present. There is nothing but God, therefore if God is for me, who can be against me?"

Today, he has proven to himself and all who know him that nothing is against him, that all things work together for good for them that love good. By having right motives and adhering steadfastly to this premise he has built up a successful business. Lacking any material capital, he invested spiritual resources and accomplished what was seemingly impossible, drawing to himself the right friends and associates who were needed. As he sat in my office a year later, he said again, "If God is for me, who can be against me?"

"Why, this applies to everyone of us in every area of our lives," I thought. Any belief of sickness, lack, or inharmony is a feeling that somewhere in life something is against us. Nothing in life is against us, therefore there is no room for discouragement.

THE PERFECT ANTIDOTE FOR DISCOURAGEMENT

Whenever you feel discouraged, sit down and put a piece of paper in front of you. If you have a specific problem, write out the problem in its entirety on one side of the paper. Then, on the other side, write out every possible solution. Really open up your mind to let the ideas come. Even if the solution that comes to you seems to be impossible, write it out. Often I have seen the *impossible* solution become the answer. Once the attention has been focused on answers the power is taken away from the problem and answers appear.

Then, take another sheet of paper, and write down all of the things that are encouraging about your life—your assets, your friends, your abilities, and such. Pour these out onto paper and keep pouring until you run dry. On the other side of the paper, write all of the discouraging things about your life. Empty them all out. After you have done this, take each one on the discouraging side and draw a line through it. Say to yourself, "I am through with this! It is not the truth about me."

Now, give all of your attention to the things that are encouraging about you and your life at the present time. That to which we give our attention grows. As we give our attention to the good, the positive, and the right, these will become our experience.

LIFE IS AN ADVENTURE

We are adventurers on the highway of life, moving from the known to the unknown. We know where we are today, our place in life, our situation, our relationships of the moment. We may know the substance of our life today; but we look ahead, thinking of tomorrow, next week, or a month or a year from today, and we cannot always see just how our lives are shaping up. As we try to imagine what we will be doing ten years from today, we have no way of knowing just what will be taking place in this changing world. But, we will know one thing for certain: there is within us the Wisdom and Power and Love of God that will never leave us or forsake us.

> Lo, I am with you always.[5] I will go before you and make the crooked places straight.[6] When thou passest through the waters, I will be with thee; and through the rivers, they shall not overflow thee: when thou walkest through the fire, thou shalt not be burned; neither shall the flame kindle upon thee.[7]

LIFE IS AN UNFOLDING PROCESS

We find ourselves sometimes moving from comparative ease to points of crises; yet, it makes no difference if we know who we are and what we have to work with. It is all part of the journey, a rough spot in the road that is soon passed and forgotten.

In the overall scheme, Life is an unfolding process, not confined to one little experience on this earth, but a Universal unfoldment of an eternal experience. Each experience has a meaning of its own, a lesson to be learned, strength to be gained, or some growth to be made that will prove valuable to us as we go along. It is still: *nothing ventured, nothing gained.* We cannot afford to become discouraged. As Robert Browning wrote in "Rabbi Ben Ezra":

> Grow old along with me!
> The best is yet to be,
> The last of life, for which the first was made:
> Our times are in His hand
> Who saith A whole I planned,
> Youth shows but half: trust God: see all nor be afraid!

[5] Matthew 28:20.
[6] Isaiah 45:2.
[7] Isaiah 43:2.

SELF-DIRECTION

I refuse to become discouraged.
Right within me is the wisdom to meet every situation.
I am led, guided, and directed to make right choices.
The Perfect Power within me knows what to do and how to do it.
Right within me is the Power to which nothing is impossible.
I trust the Perfect Power within me in all that I do.

XX CONSTANT PEACE OF MIND—THE REWARD OF GOOD SELF-DIRECTION

Nothing can bring you peace but yourself.
Nothing can bring you peace but the triumph of principles.
RALPH WALDO EMERSON

WHEN we come right down to it, the ultimate goal of most of us today is peace of mind. Some think that they will find it through renewed health; some believe that marital happiness would bring them peace; a great many believe that wealth is the sure road to peace of mind. In the mad quest for greater peace, all too many seek it through some temporary panacea such as drugs or alcohol. We have only to look around us or do a little soul-searching to find that none of these things supply that elusive goal—peace of mind.

The word peace is derived from the Latin *pacere* meaning to "make an agreement." To be centered in peace is to be in complete agreement with life. True peace of mind, the goal of every man and woman, is a state of tranquility; freedom from disturbance or agitation; being in harmony with life and those around us; a sense of calm. Each one must find his own inner peace before he can give it to another.

RESISTANCE IS MENTAL POISON

The opposite to peace of mind is conflict—inner conflict that stems from resistance of one sort or another; resisting people; resisting situations; resisting circumstances; resisting ideas. Resistance brings turmoil, chaos, and resulting stress into the life and experience of the one who entertains it. Therefore we must find an antidote for resistance if we are to ever find a lasting peace of mind.

Resistance, at the time, always seems so logical to the human mind which fails to realize that it is dealing with poison. Contrariwise, the healing power of agreement is always the way out of any difficulty. When we look away from the object of resistance and focus our attention upon the creative power of agreement, new channels of creativity are opened to us which we never dreamed were ours. Let us consider some of the aspects of agreement.

AGREEMENT WITH LIFE

To be creative, one must be in agreement with life. In looking to history, we find that some of the most creative periods in man's existence were in times of great stress and turmoil, such as a war or some other time of crisis. On the surface, this may seem to be a paradox. Yet, we find that when man is faced with an emergency, when faced with a great need, that is the time when he is more inclined toward agreement. Perhaps it is because at such a time he realizes his own inadequacy, the inadequacy of mortal man, and must reach out to a Power that is greater than he is.

A man by the name of John Flavel, back in 1690, first made the remark, "Man's extremity is God's opportunity." Since then, many others have found this truth and claimed it for their own. When man is faced with his greatest need, he turns at last to the great Power within and places himself in a point of agreement with it. Before that, he is in conflict and this causes him to have a sense of separation from life. Some doctors today are telling us that all of man's ills stem from stress. Stress is but another word for a state of being out of agreement with the Life Principle which is willing and able to bring us back into perfect harmony with health, wealth, and wisdom when we turn to It. It is easy to see that any great problem that forces us to turn, out of a sense of desperation, to the Life Principle that is all Power, agreeing with It at last, becomes a blessing in disguise. When Jesus said, *Nevertheless, Father, not my will; but thine be done,* he had overcome the world.

AGREEMENT WITH LIFE IS CREATIVITY

When we cease trying to force life to do our bidding and start agreeing with the creative Life Principle within us, letting It live through us, we are going to find ways to live a creative life. In such a life there is a sense of fulfillment. Anything that will create in the mind of an individual a sense of oneness and unity, will cause within that individual a feeling of joy and satisfaction. Whether it be by giving satisfaction through a business arrangement, painting a picture, producing beautiful music, or even baking a batch of cookies, that person feels that he is agreeing with life, he is giving to life and life is giving to him. There is no sense of separation. Then, a sense of peace reflects into every part of his life.

The man who loves his business is agreeing with life. He loves to be creative in it, to express himself through the business in such a way that people will receive satisfaction. The worker who gets satisfaction out of his work, whether he is an artisan or is working at a bench, is the person who is putting love into it. That is the reason that Paul said, *Love is the fulfilling of the law.* Love is creative, love is constructive, love is respectful—filled with respect for the thing that is being done. Love releases the Power of God, for it is God expressed in the life of man.

AGREE WITH GOD

It all amounts to agreeing with God, Infinite Goodness within us and within all of life. It means agreeing with all that God is—Life, Truth, Love, Beauty, Wisdom, Peace—the attributes of God. Believe it or not, when we contend with life in any way, we are contending with God for God is all there is. We are saying, in essence, "Why did You do this to me?" But, God, the perfect Life Principle, goes right on being perfect, beholding His creation perfect, and we, as frail mortals, beat ourselves to a pulp resisting the evil we have set up in our own minds when all the time we need only join up with the Perfection of God already established for us. It is like a bird beating vainly against a glass window when the door to freedom stands open and waiting.

How do we agree with God? Here are some examples:

AGREE WITH PEACE

It is up to us to choose. Are we going to contend with war and warmongers or are we going to find peace right where we are. Every moment that we spend resisting the wrong that is in the world today, fans the flames of war, destroys the very cells in our bodies and accomplishes not one thing for the cause of peace. This does not mean that we do not believe in principle; or that we are not willing to stand for principle. It means that we move in the direction of ideals and principles, but not against people, nor do we resist conditions. Keeping the mind centered on peace, we move forward irrespective of what may be happening around us. If one's mind is filled with thoughts of contention, wickedness in high places, evil and corruption, he is going to express such thinking in his life and affairs and in the larger life of the community. If his mind is centered on the peace of God, on justice and right action, conserving the energy that he might waste resisting conditions, he will be a strength for peace, an instrument for good right where he is. *Let there be peace and let it begin with me* is the only way to accomplish anything toward the cause of peace.

When the attention is centered on God, God and I are a majority. When the attention is centered on peace, one becomes an instrument for peace. *All power is given unto me in heaven* (within) *and in earth* [1] (the outer), said the Christ. Let's stop being little birds, beating our wings in vain attempts to get through the glass. Resistance is always destructive. A handful of people standing for peace can accomplish great things.

This applies not only to world conditions but to all the wrongs and injustices today.

RESIST NOT EVIL

Jesus was continually speaking of this. *Ye have heard that it hath been said, an eye for an eye, and a tooth for a tooth: but I say unto you, that ye resist not evil; but whosoever shall smite thee on thy right cheek, turn to him the other also. And if any man will sue thee at the law, and take away thy coat, let him have thy cloak, also. And whosoever shall compel thee to go a mile, go with him twain . . . Ye have heard that it hath been said, thou shalt love thy neighbour, and hate thine enemy. But I say unto you, love your enemies, bless them that curse you, do good to them that hate you, and pray for them which despitefully use you, and persecute you; that ye may be the children of your Father which is in heaven.*

This whole teaching is based on agreement. The one who turns the other cheek has no resentment, there is no hate, no feeling of being against; there is agreement. Where there is no resistance, the fury goes out of the antagonist. He is disarmed.

[1] Matthew 28:18.

In a book which I treasure, *The Ways and Power of Love* by Pitirim A. Sorokin,[2] many cases are given of real life incidents where love overcomes hate in wonderful ways. When thieves, surprised in the act of stealing, were offered anything they wanted, they turned away and could not steal. Torturers, who were met with love instead of resistance, no longer wanted to be cruel. "The murdered is oftentimes guilty of his own murder," said the Prophet.[3] Resistance begets resistance and all of its attendant ills; but, love overcomes hate, and good overcomes evil. It is the only way.

And if any man will sue thee at the law, and take away thy coat, let him have thy cloak also. Jesus doesn't say that you shouldn't have a lawsuit; the teaching here is that if your opponent wins at the law and takes your coat, in order not to be involved in hate or resentment, give him more. This releases any sense of hate and resentment in you.

I have twice left a successful practice of law to devote my time to teaching a philosophy of affirmative and positive living—love instead of hate; overcoming evil with good. I could show you many cases where people entered into long expensive lawsuits. They were fully justified. The law was on their side. In the end they won; but, at what a price! Many times the cost in dollars and cents was greater than the initial loss; but, the cost in health and happiness and peace of mind could never be reckoned; it was so great.

AGREE WITH GOD IN ALL OF LIFE

What is that to thee? follow thou me.[4] Agree with the Christ within, with the divine center of Love within, and do not get involved with anyone or anything. The enemies that we have in the world have to be cultivated within us. That is

---

2 Pitirim A. Sorokin, op. cit.
3 Kahlil Gibran, *The Prophet*, (New York: Alfred A. Knopf, 1958).
4 John 21:22.

what the Bible means when it says in both the Old and New Testaments, *the enemies are all those of our own households.* Once we are able to cancel them out in love, then we are going to find that there are no enemies in our experience. As you establish yourself, in consciousness, in a new life of inner peace and divine agreement, you will rise out of the former experience into a new experience. *As within, so without.* When there are no enemies in consciousness, there will be no enemies in your experience. When there is no resistance in consciousness, there will be no antagonistic people in one's experience.

Resistance is the antipathy of agreement. Resistance is the thing we have to watch more than anything else in our lives. Resisting our circumstances, resisting the people in our experience, resisting conditions, or just resisting subways or the weather. Resistance is the greatest enemy of peace of mind.

What does the word *agree* mean? It means to harmonize with, to work together, to be unified with, to be as one. When two agree, they are as one. When there is agreement within the individual, he is unified within himself and with all of life, the perfect Power now flows through him into accomplishment.

AGREEING WITH ONE'S ENVIRONMENT

Agree with the place where you live. It may not be the place where you want to live at all; but, at least you are not resisting it. You are harmonizing with it. Say to yourself, "I am in accord with life; I am in accord with this place; I am in harmony with it. I am in the right place, doing the right thing at the right time. I do not have to resist my environment because I know that that which I place in mind is sure to become my experience. I behold that which I desire and give thanks for it now, knowing that my own shall come to me."

FINDING THE GOOD IS AGREEING WITH LIFE

Let's find something good to build on in every situation. This is a wonderful way to rule out that old enemy, resistance.

In an ancient writing, the story is told of Jesus that once when he was walking along with his disciples, they came to the body of a dog by the side of the road. The dog had been dead for many days and was in an unpleasant state, to say the least. The disciples began to react to this situation as most people would, but Jesus said, "What beautiful teeth that dog had."

Try responding to good in each and every situation. Find the good. Voice no criticism nor condemnation. Try it for a week and you will find that you have opened the way to creativity. The channels are open. Nothing stands in the way. God can live through you into an expression of health and divine well-being such as you had not believed possible. A woman I know was healed of cancer when she got rid of her "little hates." That is what she called them; resistance to washing dishes was one of them. Are your resistances worth keeping? Agree with life and life will agree with you.

AGREEMENT WITH LIFE BRINGS INNER SECURITY

As we establish for ourselves new patterns of agreement we find that we are less and less prone to resist life. As we eliminate resistance we discover the peace that passes all understanding. We are no longer at the mercy of fate. A new, sure confidence takes hold of us.

Agreement is a very real thing. It makes no difference how many there may be who disagree, who are in contention, or who are striving and struggling against one. God and I are a majority.

This, then, is the answer, agreement with divine Love, the

Christ within, letting it live through us healing us of hatred, judgments, and resentments; letting it guide and instruct us in the way that we should go, taking all resistance out of everyday living, giving us freedom to live creatively and happily in any situation, giving us the power and the intelligence to reconstruct our lives into paths of peace and divine right action.

SELF-DIRECTION

I am profoundly undisturbed.

I believe in the power of good in my life.

There is no power in conditions: there is no power in personalities: there is only power in good.

There is no person, place, thing, condition, or circumstance that can interfere with the power of good within me right now.

I feel nothing done against me: nothing can disturb me.

Nothing in my past life has any power to hurt me.

I am making my future by good thinking right now.

I live in the present; I trust in the future; I have no regrets for the past.

I believe that all of life is working together for my good.

I am undisturbed. I am at peace.